THE SPENCER HAYWOOD RULE

THE SPENCER HAYWOOD RULE

BATTLES, BASKETBALL,
AND THE MAKING OF AN
AMERICAN ICONOCLAST

MARC J. SPEARS AND **GARY WASHBURN**

TRIUMPH
BOOKS

This book is available in quantity at special discounts for your group or organization. For further information, contact:

Triumph Books LLC
814 North Franklin Street
Chicago, Illinois 60610
(312) 337-0747
www.triumphbooks.com

Printed in U.S.A.
ISBN: 978-1-62937-776-6

Photos courtesy of the author unless otherwise indicated.

Design by Jonathan Hahn

This book is dedicated to my wife, Linda, and my four beautiful daughters: Zulekha, Courtney, Shaakira, and Isis. One Love.
—Spencer Haywood

This book is dedicated to my wife, Rishika; parents, Curtis and Carolyn; and my sister, Courtney. Thanks for your love and support. Special thanks to cousin Kameron Hay.
—Marc J. Spears

To my mother, Robin, and my partner, Annya. This journey, this work, would not have been possible without you.
—Gary Washburn

CONTENTS

1

COTTON

IT'S HORRIBLE TO SAY THIS, because it was definitely nightmarish to live it, but sometimes—often times in Mississippi's dark racist history—the truth hurts:

Picking cotton, basically since he was born, was the foundation for Naismith Memorial Basketball Hall of Famer Spencer Haywood becoming an elite basketball player on every level—high school, Olympic, college, ABA, and NBA.

"I came out of the cottonfields," Spencer Haywood said. "I grabbed every rebound that came off the backboard. For people to learn how to rebound, they had to work at it. But that shit was easy for me because I had been picking cotton, dragging those sacks, lifting those 100-pound sacks on my shoulders, and dumping them out. I was just cock strong.

"I didn't know it at the time, that I was in training as a player when I was picking that cotton, dragging that sack around that was 100 pounds. My legs, for a young person, were really developed."

Spencer Haywood has a loud and booming voice and a personality that can fill up any room. The first day he was heard was on April

22, 1949. This African American infant was born in a Mississippi town called Silver City that had just over 300 people claiming it as residence. Haywood's birth was not documented by the city, Humphreys County, or the State of Mississippi. Rather, a midwife wrote what would be a historic birth down in a Bible that would prove to have more importance to the United States of America than just offering the Lord's word.

"Silver City. It ain't no city, and it ain't no silver," Spencer said. "When you go outside of the little town we were living in, you're looking at about 150 people."

Unfortunately for Spencer, his dad was not there when he took his first breath.

John Haywood was from the Mississippi Hills National Heritage Area, which is in northeastern Mississippi and was named a federally designated National Heritage Area to commemorate the region's impact on the Civil War and the Civil Rights Movement. He was a sharecropper and a carpenter who was masterful with his hands. Spencer said his dad made a lucrative living building churches, businesses, and homes for "rich White folks" in the Silver City area. John was also a fair-skinned, half-Black and half-White man born from a Black mother raped by a White man, Spencer said.

John Haywood also had big dreams in the late 1940s for himself and his children that, under the circumstances, appeared to be supported by Whites in need of housing. Being half-White helped his cause.

"He could build anything," Spencer said. "'I had my boys. We'll have my company and we're gonna be *the shit*.' He built houses, churches, Leroy's Café. He just built it and other farmhands would help him on the side when he got out of the field. They needed him, and he was also half-White."

Mr. John was actually doing extremely well for a Black man typically with the most limited of opportunities in a racist state, where many White men had little regard for people of his skin tone. While carpenter John Haywood certainly had the ability to build a large home for his family of nine kids alongside a dirt road, he also had the intelligence to realize it was better to limit his to three bedrooms to keep the local Whites from jealousy and potential retaliation.

"You can't build too big because you can't overshadow the people who had less," Spencer said. "You couldn't shine on the White folks because they would burn it down."

The stories Spencer Haywood speaks of his father now are not personal experience.

"I didn't know nothing about my father," Spencer said.

Why?

John Haywood actually died of a heart attack at age 64 in Silver City about three weeks before his future basketball star son was born. With the unexpected death of her husband, Eunice Haywood instantly became a single mother with her ninth child in baby Spencer, who was born prematurely by help of a midwife on his parent's bed. She would have later give birth to two more kids, but she vowed never to marry again due to her love for John Haywood.

"He was working on a home and he just fell and had a heart attack," Spencer said about his father. "My mother was pregnant with me. It was a traumatic experience for me losing him and I am inside her kicking to get out. So I came on the scene a little early. We couldn't go to no doctors. A midwife brought me into the world on the same bed that I was conceived. My mom was worried about this baby because he was puny."

John Haywood actually never took part in sharecropping, according to Spencer, because the demand of his buildings was too high and lucrative. Spencer says the family would have been "rich" in a major Mississippi town if his father never passed away.

"My mom would say that [would have happened] if my father would have moved us to Yazoo City or Jackson, where they really could use his work," Spencer said. "He had his whole crew built-in with six boys."

Spencer said that he considered his tough, hard-working, older field hand, 6-foot-4 brother, Joe; his older brother, Andrew; and neighbor and field hand M.H. Ratliff as his main "father figures." But ultimately, it was his mother, Eunice Haywood, who raised him and gave him his first dose of confidence.

"From jump street she always believed in me," Spencer said. "I get emotional when I think about. She would always say I was replacing John as the breadwinner."

Eunice Haywood was from Kosciusko, a small town in central Mississippi built along the Natchez trace that was used by Native Americans and European settlers. Today, the central Mississippi town of close to 7,500 people is more famous for being the birthplace of famed television host and actress Oprah Winfrey and Civil Rights figure James Meredith.

The dark-skinned Black and Native American woman was involved in sharecropping her entire life. She had to drop out of school when she was in the fourth grade so she could sharecrop.

One of Eunice Haywood's two previous children prior to meeting her husband came from a rape from White men, Spencer said.

John and Eunice Haywood also didn't meet organically at church, concert, or some speakeasy for Blacks in the Silver City area. According to Spencer Haywood, White male farmers that ran the cotton fields in Silver City recruited them to work there. He also said that the White male farmers pushed his tall parents to date in hopes of them re-producing large and tall children.

John came to the union with two children already: his daughter, Ollie Mae, and his son, AW. Eunice also already had two daughters, Virgal Lee and Lena Mae. Once they were married, they had (in birth order) son Joe, son Leroy, son Andrew, daughter Lavaughn, Spencer, son Floyd, and daughter Ivory.

"This White farmer was trying to get some farm people to do the work," Spencer said. "My mom and dad met on 'Goat Hill'—about eight miles outside of Silver City—where there was farming of real raw cotton. They met there. They were indentured slaves. They were actually put together by the farmers.

"My mom was tall, about 5'9". My dad was 6'4". Two big, strong Blacks. 'If we can get those two together, they can create some kids that would be great for this farm.' They could do all of the work. They were not forced, but they got together out of necessity. Either you work and survive or you perish. The ruling class had them under their thumb. You had to go with it. It was modern-day slavery."

Spencer Haywood continued to be literally close to his mother after his birth, as he was swaddled to her back wherever she went after being born prematurely. She was very worried about her premature son and rubbed dandelion and burdock root on him "to heal and bring back to life," Spencer said.

Spencer Haywood believed as far back as he could remember that he would be someone special in life because his mother treated him that way.

"She nursed this baby back to life," Spencer said. "My aunt Harriet, who is no longer living, told me these long stories about my mother. Because my father had died, my mother flipped her energy into me like, 'This is going to be our special one.' I grew up with the idea that I was going to do something special and something deep. All I had to do was survive and don't let nobody shoot you or hang you.

"She was always a little bit extra protective. And I played on it, too… I remember people talking about how I wouldn't give up the tit. I hung up in there. I knew I was different because she treated me different. I knew it was because of a traumatic experience, but I didn't realize it. I just thought I was a special person."

Most of that time was spent in nearby cotton fields as his mother worked primarily as a sharecropper and also as a domestic servant. She worked about 18 hours a day , and there was still never more than 24 in it. While slavery was over, the rural South was known for having former slaves and generations of their kin out in the blazing sun working on fields picking cotton. Spencer said the typical wages in the early 1950s at the Goat Hill Cotton Farm where his mother worked was $2 per day, working from sun up to sun down. Children were paid $1.50 per day.

The Goat Hill Cotton Farm was owned by Albert Heidelberg, who Spencer says was great to work for because "he didn't hassle you." Overseer John Quinn, who was half-White and half-Black, however, was very hard on the workers and was a "taskmaster," according to Spencer. Spencer believed that John Quinn's mother was raped by a farmer and he was in charge because he was "closer to the master" race wise. Spencer said that his brother Andrew looked up to Quinn and aspired to be like him.

"He was serious about getting his 'niggers' to work and getting the best product," Spencer said.

Spencer's youngest recollection of Goat Hill was riding on his mother's cotton sack as an infant. He said at age three he learned how to pick the cotton that was low by the ground and put it into a sack. Even at that young age, Spencer viewed picking cotton as his job and actually initially thought it was "great," because he didn't know any better than those horrible and hot working conditions.

"The sun was beaming down. The planes were spraying us with DDT [pesticide] to kill the weeds and boll weevil," Spencer said. "But there was 50 to 100 people out there and they were singing spirituals, work songs. And it's a rhythm and a cadence to it. As a kid you're thinking, 'Whoa, this shit is so cool and so great. It's awesome.' But as an adult, you think they're just killing themselves. The planes were coming over our heads. The farmers would say, 'It ain't gonna hurt you. We're just gonna kill the insects so you niggers stay in the field and hit the ground.'

"We would hit the ground, put our hand to our head and the plan would fly right over us spraying all that shit, chemicals. They weren't spraying at night because it wasn't that kind of respect. 'These are my slaves so I can do whatever I want to do.' And to be honest, they didn't know they were killing us. They were saying, 'My grandpa did it like this, so this is how I'm gonna do it.'"

Spencer said that his mother also moonlighted as a caretaker for the farmers in the town once things started slowing down in the cotton fields. She was a great cook and enjoyed cooking for the White people in town. Spencer said, "Once the field was weak she raised the White folks and she raised us."

But even after Spencer Haywood made it big in pro basketball, his mother continued to work in the cotton fields and cooked and cleaned for White people because she did not want to come off as a "prima donna lady."

"She could not leave the fields," Spencer said. "It's too hard sitting at home. Everyone else [Black] is all out in the fields. That is all she grew up with. So, she would just go help them pick and do stuff. 'I want to keep my church members happy. I don't want them to think I am some prima donna lady.' It didn't bother me because I knew that was what she wanted.

"When I first made some money, I came down and said, 'Mom, I'm gonna build this house.' I was talking to my brothers Floyd and Andrew about how I want to put a whirlpool in the house and all this… and she said, 'What are y'all talking about. I do not want no house like that. I want my house no house bigger than the people of my church or I am going to make the White folks mad.'"

Spencer ended up building a three-bedroom home for his mother. But she would later tell him that he should have convinced her to get a bigger house. He also sent her money during his pro career that she put in the bank in preparation of him becoming "broke." Spencer said that his family members eventually "wiped her out" of the money he gave her.

Haywood said that the sharecroppers would always get sick after a big pesticide spraying. But did they ever complain? Not unless they wanted a death wish. And life-threatening actions was not limited to just sharecropping Blacks.

"If you complained, they would say, 'What the hell's wrong with you?' Then you would be shot right on the spot. Dead. I saw all of that shit," Spencer said. "When guys left Mississippi and came back and farmers would see them and say, 'Hey boy, what you doing back here?' And then they were like, 'Don't call me boy.' And then you knew they were going to try to hang this person at night.

"The sheriff was the Ku Klux Klan. All the White farmers and people around were the Klan. And they had their meetings at their lodges, churches."

Spencer said he was 6-foot-1 at age 14. Due to his height, strength, and long arms, he was able to make 25 cents more per day than the other kids on the cotton fields in a role as a "step puller." Workers were transported on big trucks that had two rows of seats in the bed. When the trucks picked up the workers in the morning, the step pullers jump off the truck once it made its stop, put down "big iron steps" and aided the elderly or anyone else that needed help up the steps. Step pullers also had to get up earlier than the workers to be ready to help the workers on to the trucks.

Spencer described being a step puller as a "pride job" and still "my best job ever" due to some of the perks it offered.

"I would say, 'C'mon, let me help you up here.' So, you would put everyone on the truck and yell up at the driver, 'Go 'head!' and we'd pull out and go on to the next stop," Spencer said. "I was tall and I really wanted that job because it took off my field time. The workers respected me because I really loved that job. I loved that shit. I know it's crazy. We would put all the people into the truck and go on to the field."

Spencer said that he would use his premature birth story to help him in the cotton fields as well by telling the overseer that "my mom said I was sickly." Once he became a step puller, he used that old story to help him get the job of bringing water to the workers. Spencer had rivalries with his brothers. And after landing this posh gig, he made time to taunt his brothers and sisters working in the fields.

"I thought I had died and went to heaven," Spencer said. "I got the water boy job. I would sit in the truck, bullshitting around or go help on something, and then I would walk up to my brothers and say, 'You slaves!' And then go back in the truck."

Spencer said he took his water boy job very seriously and made the drinking water for the workers "perfect." He would chop up the ice and cool down water by dropping it in. He would make sure it was clean by making sure none of the tobacco chewers allowed any of their snuff to fall in, and he'd clean off any debris they left behind.

"The older ladies would say, 'Boy, this is the best water that I had in 20 years,'" Spencer said with a smile. "I kept my water at a pristine level."

Meanwhile, John Quinn the overseer was taking notice on how tall, big, and strong Spencer was getting. He did not understand why one of the young strong boys with height and super long arms was not working in the field. Spencer was "crushed" when, at 12, his step pulling days were over, as Quinn put him back in the cotton fields.

To retaliate in his own special way, Spencer said he would sing songs about freedom for a fictional person named Matt Lucas. Singing a song about someone who did not exist kept him from getting literally killed by Quinn.

"My theme song was, 'One of these days, and it won't be long, you are gonna be looking for Matt Lucas and Matt Lucas would be gone,'" Spencer said. "Matt Lucas was me. All I did back then was listen to the radio at night. We didn't have a television. 'You are listening to WLAC out of Nashville.' It would go on to New Orleans.

"The Blues disc jockeys would be talking shit. And I would mimic them and that's how I came up with the name 'Matt Lucas.' I couldn't say my name or they were gonna shoot me. So, that was my theme song. Matt was always planning to get out of Mississippi."

Spencer would eventually find some other side jobs to make money around age 12. He says he became a bootleg barber. After his brother Andrew fixed a lawn mower, he made money moving lawns. He said he also put money in on furniture his family bought for the house as a pre-teen.

"I bought my family the first TV we ever had at the age of 12," Spencer said.

From time to time, Spencer said that his family would see dead Black people who were hanged to death in Silver City for "retaliatory verbiage." With each sighting, his mother gave her children a "life and death" warning. Spencer said that Black folks in Silver City were also scared to vote for fear of being punished by White people.

"She would say, 'That is what you get when you when you go talking back to these people,'" Spencer said his mother would say. "'These people are cruel and inhuman. You have to always remember to keep your mouth shut because it's always life and death.'

"I would always put my head down when I saw someone dead. You knew the people that were [hanged], shot, or put in the Yazoo river and drowned. They just come and got them."

The Haywoods lived in a small three-bedroom shotgun house. One luxury that Spencer had was that their father had left his family an acre of land to farm. What was not luxury was the multi-purpose tub that the entire family used for bathing and more.

"This was not just a bathtub," Spencer said. "We washed clothes in that tub. If you were lucky you could jump in there after all that Clorox was used. You boiled the water on the stove to put in the tub. You had to first cut the wood, put it on the stove, and boil it.

"You had to do three rounds of bathing, also. The older guys got the first round, and I was always second in the tub and the water was always dirty when it got to Floyd. I tried to dirty that shit up for him."

Spencer said there was also a box-shaped outhouse. The Haywood's used pages from the Sears, Roebuck catalogs as toilet paper. There was always a fear of being bit in the rear by snakes. They also had a pig pen with hogs attracted to the outhouse as well for different reasons.

"We had two or three pigs we were raising for a slaughter," Spencer said. "Every once in a while, one would escape and we would panic saying, 'What are we gonna do? The pig is gone. Mama gonna kill us.' She would always say, 'The pig ain't going nowhere. The pig is in the outhouse eating shit. So go on get it….'

"You would get the pig, put them back in the pen. You couldn't wait to kill them."

Well, actually, the Haywoods themselves did not lead the charge on killing the pigs. There was a Black man who specialized in slaughtering, who wasn't viewed as the most attractive man, and who had a nickname to second that notion.

"His name was 'Booty Face,'" Spencer said. "I can't remember his real name. But we called him, 'Booty Face,' because his face looked like a booty. We didn't know his name so we called him, 'Mr. Booty Face.' We would say, 'Hey, Mr. Booty Face!'

"I didn't know his name. None of the kids knew his name. So, he accepted that as his name."

Long before the pigs were slaughtered, Mr. Booty Face would stop by the Haywood household to castrate the male piglets. According to the Literature Review on the Welfare Implications of Swine Castration, the castration of male piglets is a common in the United States "to avoid boar taint in the meat of sexually mature male pigs and to reduce aggression toward other pigs and caretakers." Mr. Booty Face was actually more worried about eating a pig delicacy than being called a derogatory name. He loved to eat sautéed pig testicles.

Spencer said that he and his siblings got a kick out of watching Mr. Booty Face castrate their piglets two to three at time. And after, Spencer said Mr. Booty Face would ask his mother for a pan to fry the testicles with some salt and pepper for his immediate consumption. And he would not share one bite with anyone.

"He would eat them right in front of us," Spencer said. "We would say to each other, 'When are we gonna eat some of those oysters.' He would talk about them with such regard. He would say, 'Well, kids when you grow up this is what you're gonna get. You will get taste of these oysters.' We would say, 'Can we taste them, sir? Can we see what they are like?' 'Nah, these are mine.' He was cooking them right there and eating them.

"We would be sitting there salivating and thinking, 'One of these days we're gonna get us some hog nuts!' I ate them years later. It was not bad. It was like eating a mussel."

Mr. Booty Face would also show back up to the Haywood house when the hogs were mature enough for slaughter. The Haywood kids were bittersweet about this moment since they had raised the pigs themselves. Spencer said the pigs were in the pen eating anything they threw in there before growing up to be very large. All the Black neighbors would get word that a pig was going to be slaughtered and would stop by in hopes of a cut after helping the process, Spencer said.

"All the neighbors would say is, 'Killing time at the Haywood's,'" Spencer said. "Everyone participated and Mr. Booty Face was the man in charge. That was his time to really show his skills. He was like a hero, in a way. You would sit and think, *Man, Mr. Booty Face is gonna kill a hog I raised.* Mr. Booty Face would say, 'Pet him,' to get them all relaxed. So, you would think, *What is he gonna do? Is he gonna shoot them?* No, he's not gonna shoot them. He had the back of his axe over his head and then he would stand over the hog and hit him right on his nose.

"Bam! Bust his head open. He would not mess up too much of the head because you wanted to eat it. Then he would slit his neck with a knife, tie his legs up and pull him up with a pulley. And the blood would run out and then we get to skin it. My brothers, Floyd and Andrew; my sisters, Lavaughn and Ivory; and me, we were into that shit. And we were working with Booty Face! This is classic shit. We would get the hog all cleaned up and drop him into a barrel. We would scrape all his hair off and my mother would be trying to figure out something to do with the hair because she hated to throw away anything on a hog."

Spencer said his family would eat the meat from a hog for several weeks, keeping it fresh in an ice box. The Haywoods, however, would also put all their excess meat into a smokehouse on their property. Smokehouses are used to keep heat and smoke inside while keeping out most airflow. A typical smokehouse was used to smoke meats, chicken, and fish, so it could be eaten at a later time without rotting.

"You put the meat cured with salt in the smokehouse, like they do in Italy, hanging from a string," Spencer said. "This food is not to be eaten until needed. The preacher would come by on the first Sunday, and we would break him a piece. But when we were really starving, we would break into the smokehouse and get the ham."

Spencer said that the Haywoods were predominately "self-sufficient" as they also grew vegetables on their property for their consumption. They grew corn, okra, tomatoes, watermelons, and more. They also preserved leftover vegetables in jars for times when food was scarce. They purchased very little food after receiving their allotment of "commodity food." In other words, welfare food given to them by the State of Mississippi.

Mama Haywood wouldn't allow her children to get their commodity food without pride, despite the embarrassment it brought.

"We were so poor," Haywood said. "We would go eight miles and the state would give us a basket of food. We were so embarrassed. The kids would know when we were going and say, 'Ha, they're going to the commodity store to get some food.' My mom would make us stand up in the truck we got a ride on. You had to have pride to get this food.

"We would get bologna, grits, commodity cheese, and canned meat. We did not know what kind of meat that was. But it was good shit when you do not have anything. We would go through that and the cheese fast because [us kids] were growing."

The Haywoods also raised chickens after they received a box of chicks from Nashville in the mail. Actually, Spencer's mom gave him the responsibility of being in charge of raising the chickens. It was another example of Spencer being treated special by his mother, and he didn't want to disappoint.

Spencer fed them with ground corn to keep them from choking, and kept them in a cage. Spencer earned the nickname "Weddie," which he still responds to today from family members, while he raised the chickens as a kid. Spencer said the best thing his mom cooked was fried chicken with a side of rice and gravy.

"When they chicklets got out and ran around, my mom, Miss Eller across the street, and my next door neighbor would yell, 'Get the little chicken, Weddie! Weddie, Weddie, Weddie!'" Spencer said. "I would equate that to the chickens because I was young. The chickens and me were one. I would run and get them and put them back in the cage. Everyone would say, 'That's his name: Weddie.'

"When they got a little size on them, all your great work would go up in smoke because she would grab one by the next and snap his head. She would say, 'We got a Sunday meeting at church and we're going to eat good this weekend.' She would snap his head. The chicken would be jumping around dead. You'd be like, 'Goddamn.' But it would be some good shit to eat."

Spencer said that the Haywood boys would also hunt wild animals and fish in Mississippi for food. They would hunt rabbits, but if you got the ones with worms in their necks it would ruin that catch. When rabbit hunting season was bad, he said they would put on hats with lights on them to hunt in the dark. They would hunt for frogs and raccoons.

"Raccoon is stringy, but it wasn't bad with gravy and rice," Spencer said.

Spencer said in the wintertime, when the Haywoods were "starving" and struggling to get meat, the kids would go to the graveyards to hunt possum. They would kill the slow possums with sticks. From there, Spencer's mother would clean the possum and cook it for the family.

"We would kill it by busting it in the head with a stick," Spencer said. "We had a gun, but we couldn't blow his head off because we would mess up all the meat. We weren't going to waste bullets from a 20-gauge or 12-gauge on no possum. If you scared him, he would act like he was going to bite you. Then he would lay down and act like he was dead, which [is where you get] 'playing possum.'

"Then we would bust that bastard in his head and come home and eat it. It did not taste that good because you knew he was in the graveyard getting down in the ground and eating human bodies. And you could always find them on the highways eating roadkill."

The family would also eat roadkill if the animal was killed recently. The only roadkill they drew the line at were dogs. They would occasionally add boiled or scrambled eggs with the wild meats to add.

"If it was on the road and it was fresh, it was going into our pot," Haywood said. "I know it was bad, but there was something intriguing about it. We were hunters. My sisters were like, 'My brothers are nasty and horrible.' But they would eat it [too] because we had nothing else to eat."

Spencer Haywood has enjoyed the some of the best restaurants in the United States and internationally, but when it comes to the best food he has ever eaten, his first choice was his mom's cooking, no matter how exotic it was.

"There was nothing ever better. Very few things in life were better than what I ate there," Spencer said. "Even all that exotic shit."

2

GROWING UP IN MISSISSIPPI

COTTON IN MISSISSIPPI IS TYPICALLY PLANTED in late-April, with the flower blooming in mid-June and harvesting in the fall in late-September and October.

And when it was not cotton-picking or chopping season, Spencer went to school. Spencer said going to school was "the coolest thing," because he didn't have to be in the cotton fields.

He went to an all-Black public school for kids in Silver City that went through the eighth grade. The school was paid for by the State of Mississippi and was about three miles from his family home in Old Town. It was built like a shotgun house with classes on each side. The school had a tough female "taskmaster," as Spencer called the principal, who would discipline children by spanking them with a belt and a "big ol' paddle."

There was a bus that took the children in his neighborhood to the school, but if they missed it there was literally a mad dash to get there before the first bell in hopes of avoiding the punishment.

"You had to run to get there," Spencer said. "It would happen if we were slow coming out of the house. 'Oh, my pants were not pressed right.' Or arguing over bullshit. My older brother Andrew loved to miss school, so sometimes we followed the big leader in chief—the John Quinn look-alike. We would end up being late or missing school. There would be an ass-whooping once we got to school and an ass-whooping when we got home.

"We would run to school in hopes of passing the bus. We would clock out and walk after two-and-a-half miles."

Spencer said that he and his fellow Black students were given old books that the area White schools discarded. A lot of the books had writing in them. Spencer said some of the books even had racist words like "Niggas" written inside from racist White students who had used them previously. Spencer added that the history books were "slanted" toward a racist White view on history. Moreover, he said they were only taught limited mathematics because of fear that an educated sharecropper would leave the field.

"When they taught you English, they called in 'Ang-lish,'" Spencer said.

Spencer's mother did not want her children, especially the boys, going too far away from home in their free time. She would not allow them to go to neighboring towns for fear of them getting in trouble and crossing paths with racist Whites who may want to harm them. And one of the ways Spencer and his siblings stayed entertained was by playing an interesting form of basketball outside their home for entertainment.

Spencer's older brother Andrew made a much larger than usual rim out of the iron surrounding a barrel. The rim was initially connected to an electrical line, but Andrew quickly realized that electrocution and death could come with that idea. So instead, Andrew dug a hole in the ground, inserted a tall pole and attached the barrel rim about 10 feet high to it. Spencer said his mom made her children a basketball out of cotton, a croker sack, and rags. Unfortunately, with no air in it, it could not be dribbled. Spencer says he was nine years old when this first introduction to the game of basketball arrived.

"The ball couldn't bounce. So we had rules set up: 'Bop, bop, make the pass or take the shot,'" Spencer said. "We didn't have no TV, nor knew anything about basketball [history]. But we wanted to play it."

Spencer said the neighborhood boys also played baseball in the nearby cow pasture. But after being hit hard by a purposely wild pitch in the latest episode of his somewhat healthy sibling rivalry with his brother Andrew, he decided to stick to hoops.

"I got beaned by my own brother. I was up to bat and Andrew decided to hit me and he clocked me," Spencer said. "Baseball? I do not want to play against my brother. Everywhere I went, Andrew was there to challenge my life. But it was cool. I liked it."

Spencer truly fell in love with basketball at his elementary school, as it had an actual backboard and a rim at the regulation height. There were also real basketballs to use. The court, however, was a "dust bowl," as no concrete was laid for these Black children in the rural Deep South. Spencer said he enjoyed playing on the school's team that played against other local Black schools.

"We had balls that we could bounce," Spencer said. "We had full courts on both ends."

Humphreys County Country Club is a Professional Golfers Association registered golf course in Silver City. Built in 1950, according to

Golfnow.com, it is a Par 36, nine-hole golf course that is 3,165 yards and used by golfers of all levels. But when Spencer worked there from ages nine to 14, Blacks could work there but could not play.

While Spencer became an avid golfer as an adult, he has no interest in returning to this course, the home of so many racist memories.

"It was an interesting place," Spencer said.

Spencer got a job as a caddie working at the golf course through his brother Andrew, who was a groundskeeper. It was within walking distance of their house, and both boys were able to work there during the down season of cotton picking. Spencer would make $1 or $2 per day as a caddie, while he also cleaned golf shoes and golf clubs.

Spencer played golf cross-handed as a kid because he was a left-handed golfer with no golf clubs to use. To this day, he still plays golf cross-handed. Quietly, southpaw Spencer and these Black boys snuck in rounds of golf when the coast was clear, as well playing on a three-hole golf course they made nearby at a cow pasture.

"The White men would say, 'If I ever see one of y'all using my golf clubs I will kill you.' And we couldn't wait to touch the golf clubs. We would play. We would wait until they were leaving the golf club and going home and then we would go play," Spencer said. "We had to clean them anyway, so we would use their clubs and wear their shoes. We were kids. We would say, 'They're not gonna kill us. I think.' But we ain't gonna get caught one way or another. I would have run to the river road. They ain't killing me."

There was no caddie shack for these young Black caddies. So Spencer and the other young Black boys got shade and rest sitting in tall bushes until they got the racist yell for their services.

"'We need one caddie, nigger,'" Spencer recalled.

As soon as the racist request was made, several of the young Black boys would come running for duty in hopes of being picked. They would all sell themselves to be picked by the golfer. Spencer did his best to sell the golfers on his service, and boy did he ever go to all the possible lengths to please the White golfer while putting himself in harm's way.

"As kids you would try to see yourself as 'I'm gonna be the best caddie that you ever seen today,' so you could get picked," Spencer said. "My thing was service, and I tried to get a reputation for it. I would give them cold water. And if they hit a ball into a creek I would dive in there and get it. I'd jump right in with water moccasins crawling all around. I quiver when I think about it. They would tell me, 'Don't worry. A snake cannot bite you in the water.' But I went and got that golf ball."

A mixed-race man named Willie Harris was in charge of the Black caddies. Spencer said that Harris' father was White and impregnated his Black mother through rape. Mixed-race leaders of Black workers was a common theme of Spencer's childhood. The Black boys were not allowed to go into the "Whites-only" clubhouse because of the color of their skin. They were allowed to buy snacks through a window. A Black woman named Frankie used to cook the food at the golf course. She would also give food to the young Black boys working there.

Another event that stuck with Spencer was the aftermath of the Kennedy assassination.

John F. Kennedy and the Kennedy family were in favor of the Civil Rights Movement in 1960. Robert Kennedy once helped Civil Rights Leader Dr. Martin Luther King Jr. get out of jail when he was arrested after leading a protest in Atlanta. That move was an endorsement from the Kennedy's of Dr. King to the ire of the racist White Southerners.

Almost 70 percent of African Americans voted to help John F. Kennedy, a White man, become the president of the United States in a very close election in 1960. Once president, JFK gave a record number of high-level positions in his administration to Blacks, improved the Civil Rights Commission, and spoke in favor of school desegregation, praising those who aided it. President Kennedy also appointed vice president Lyndon Johnson to head up the President's Committee on Equal Employment Opportunity. Kennedy sparked major civil rights legislation to the Congress to guarantee Blacks equal access to public facilities while also pushing to end segregation in education and provide federal protection of the right to vote.

In August of 1963, King and more than 200,000 Americans of all races joined the famous "March on Washington for Jobs and Freedom." The 100-year anniversary of the Emancipation Proclamation took place at the march as well. United States president Abraham Lincoln signed the Emancipation Proclamation, or Proclamation 95, on January 1, 1863, which was a presidential proclamation and executive order to make 3.5 million enslaved African Americans free.

It was at the March on Washington that King gave his renowned "I Have A Dream," speech. Three months later, President Kennedy was assassinated while sitting in a car during a parade in Dallas.

Back at the Humphreys County Country Club, the racist White members were overheard by the Black workers celebrating Kennedy's assassination. Spencer said this golf course was used and run at this time by members of the Ku Klux Klan and other racist White members.

"They were saying, 'Yahoo, they killed that nigger lover,'" Spencer said.

Spencer said that some of the racist White members, many of who were drunk, told the young Black caddies to go onto the golf course and stand across about 50–75 yards away in a line on the same day of Kennedy's assassination. Spencer said that they told the Black boys, "We're gonna see how fast you are." There is not a driving range at the Humphreys Country Club Course. But on the same day that Kennedy was murdered, Spencer said drunk racist White members hit golf balls at the young Black boys, including himself.

Spencer said the terrifying driving range incident continued until they hit a couple of the kids, including his brother Floyd in the leg. Spencer said one kid may have received brain damage after being hit in the head by a flying golf ball.

"They were drunk and yelling, 'Yahoo,' and shit," Spencer said. "They're driving the balls at us and we're jumping and rolling to keep from getting hit. If you got hit, you just rolled with the ball. I did not get tagged. But one guy got tagged in the head. That was not cool. It was like a *pop*. It was a serious pop. We were like, 'Oh my God, he really got hit.' That ball was coming really fast. Hooking. Slicing. The golf ball was hard. His head blew up.

"We took him by his house. His father was so mad, but he could not do anything about it. But he was angry at the kid. He said, 'Why didn't you get out of the way like the rest of the boys?' If his father had showed anger to the White men, they would have killed him. I always thought the kid was a little mentally light after that."

Spencer said there were other occasions at the golf course where racist golfers might hit a young Black boy caddie with a ball or a club if they were not playing well. Spencer said he got hit a couple times by golfers.

"It's not the golfer. It's the caddie's fault. And if they had a bad shot, they would hit you with the head of the club and say, 'Fucking nigger,'" Spencer said. "If I got hit, I would say, 'I will make sure you don't hit it in that bad spot no more, sir.'"

Spencer said that he has never had nightmares or Post-Traumatic Stress Disorder from all the racist and violent things he witnessed during his youth. He said his mother's calming words helped him overcome it all and rationalize the racism.

"Every time something went down, she would say, 'Baby, the Devil has got their heart. They are good people. But the Devil has got their heart,'" Spencer said. "We rationalized everything with God and the Devil. It was a serious way of living. But that was your salvation. And if you tried to see it any other way, you could get killed. She said that with everything.

"She would say, 'Remember Weedie, those people are pretty good. I worked with them in their house. I can eat what I want. They give y'all food. They even gave y'all some clothing last year.' It was her way of protection. She did not want her girls to be raped or boys to be killed. But she also let them know, 'If you harmed one of my children, we got a shotgun, the whole town is going to blow up and we are going to kill y'all because we know y'all will want to kill us.' She would act like she was crazy to warn them."

Spencer said extremely facetiously that his oldest brother Leroy got the "short stick" by having to move from Mississippi to Detroit to help one of his aunts. Leroy was an All-State basketball player in Michigan while playing for a high school in Detroit. Spencer ended up getting motivation to work on his basketball skills after his brother mailed a newspaper clipping of his press exploits.

It was at that point that Spencer realized that he could use the game of basketball to leave Mississippi.

"That is when I said, 'Aha. I'm getting out of Mississippi. Matt is getting out of town,'" Spencer said. "That's when I really started playing. I just loved it. When people quit for the day, I kept playing. I got good at it at a young age."

Aiding Spencer's basketball game was that he was 6-foot-2 in the eighth grade. He arrived at McNair High School in Belzoni, Mississippi, standing 6-foot-6. McNair boys' head basketball Charles H. Wilson recruited Spencer as a freshman. Spencer made the varsity team, but his basketball skills had not quite adapted to his height. Making it tougher was that Spencer was playing in cheap Army shoes his mom bought him, which made him "look country." Moreover, Spencer had to wear the road uniform when the team was at home and vice versa because he was the 13th player on a team with 12 uniforms.

"Boy, was I horrible," Spencer said. "All my skills fell away with the growth. I could not do anything right. But the coach stuck with me and said, 'You're going to be my guy.'"

Coach Wilson had big dreams for Spencer and offered big support.

He bought Spencer his first pair of real basketball shoes. Not only that, Coach Wilson and the band teacher took turns driving Spencer seven miles back home after practices. Coach also spoke about his expectations of Spencer playing college basketball somewhere in Mississippi, like Alcorn State. And he told Spencer that he could be the best rebounder the school had ever had.

Basketball had the added benefit of taking Spencer outside of Humphreys County, where Silver City was located, for the first time in his life.

"He just saw this big kid," Spencer said. "He would say, 'This guy is going to be a star. He is going to be playing at Alcorn State.' I wanted to go on to Jackson State or Mississippi State. That would have been Godly. He had me dreaming."

Spencer said during his freshman year he was able to put on a regular uniform and start for the first time after one of his teammates was arrested. McNair was playing against Gentry High School from Indianola, Mississippi, that starred 6'10" center Sam Lacey. Lacey would go on to play college ball at New Mexico State and professionally in the NBA for the Cincinnati Royals, Kansas City Kings, New Jersey Nets, and Cleveland Cavaliers.

Spencer said that Lacey spit on him during the jump ball, but he was so excited about starting that he just wiped it off. Spencer got the ball after the tip and took off, dribbling strong toward the basket unopposed.

"I get the ball and I try to figure out why nobody is fouling me after I dribbled toward the rim," Spencer said. "I'm dribbling and I'm gonna lay this up perfectly. And everyone in the gym started booing. Then I looked over to my sister Laverne, who was a big supporter in the stands. She had her head down and was looking like, 'No he did not.'

"I had scored in the wrong basket. I was too excited. I just headed back down the court. My first high school basket was in the wrong basket. I shook it off. Then the coach came over and said, 'Shake it off. Shake it off. Shake it off. Shake it off. That ain't nothing. I've seen every player that was excited about the game do that.'

"Everyone was laughing at me. They said, 'Look at that tall motherfucker with that little ass head.'"

Spencer shook it off, and he got better—fast.

Spencer says he had a breakthrough game as a freshman with 15 rebounds and 10 points. Suddenly, he was treated differently at school by everyone but his jealous brother, Andrew. Spencer had a crush on a beautiful upper classmate named Barbara Holmes, who suddenly noticed him after he started succeeding on the hardwood in high school.

"I used to look at her and say, 'Boy, I wish I could kiss her,'" Spencer said. "She came up to me and said, 'You did really good.' I damn near pissed on myself and died. And when I came into class, my boys said, 'Spencer you did all that in the game?' I said, 'Yeah, I did.' I liked that feeling.

"Right when school was over, I went right to the gym and I was an hour earlier than everyone else. I was working on my game. I was running up and down the court and doing things."

Spencer said that he would often play his older brother Andrew in one-on-one before practices. Andrew had given up on basketball to concentrate on being a mechanic (he often fixed his teachers' cars), but he could still hoop. It was on the basketball court where Andrew would ultimately give his improving younger brother some well-earned respect.

"We were just balling. It was like blood and guts. Life and death. He was like, 'You didn't quite get me, but you're close,'" Spencer said.

There was a basketball buzz about Spencer after his big 15-rebound, 10-point game. Locals started paying attention to him and saying he could be even better this his older brother Leroy, who was up North in Detroit. Meanwhile, his mother was proud and added to her son's confidence boost.

"Everyone around town was talking and saying, 'He could be better than Leroy,'" Spencer said. "My mother cooked me some food and said, 'I always knew it.' That was some good shit, man."

Haywood continued to work at the golf course after he entered high school. Now 14 years old, unusually tall at 6'6" and growing, he used to entertain the golfers by showing how high he could jump by touching a mark that was hard to reach. The golfers responded with a half-compliment, half-racist insult.

"'Boy, look at Weedie. He can jump like a fucking monkey,'" Spencer said.

Meanwhile, Spencer said Willie Harris got jealous of the adulation he was receiving from the White members for his athleticism. Spencer believes Harris was in his sixties at the time. So, Harris conjured a plan to make Spencer look bad by nailing a quarter down to the floor and asking him to get it. Spencer says he attempted to snatch the quarter, but it did not budge since it was nailed to the floor. Spencer then said that Harris accused him of trying to steal his coin and slapped him.

An irate then-14-year-old Spencer began crying following this incident in 1964, which put a damper in his growing glowing reputation for being a budding local basketball star. Next ensued an argument and a fight between Spencer and Harris that wildly went into the clubhouse of the golf course.

"I lost it. I had been suppressing my feelings for so long with so much shit going on," Spencer said. "So I went after this old man. He started yelling, 'He's trying to kill me! Call the Goddamn police!' The White women in the pool were alarmed and they came out."

The local sheriff arrived shortly after and arrested Spencer. Spencer said he spent the night in jail over the incident with Harris. Even before being jailed, Spencer and his mother had a growing fear that he could get in further trouble with the local racist White men thirsty to make a buck off this growing giant. They could care less that Spencer had basketball star potential; they were thinking about his potential to help them.

"One of the things the farmers did down South in my neck of the woods, if you were growing big and strong, they would mess you up some kind of way to where you can get attacked and go to jail for two or three months and then you are relegated to that farm," Spencer said. "And that's slavery forever."

Spencer's mom ended up getting the 14-year-old inmate out of jail the next morning. He described his overnight stint in jail as "the hardest night." She made a point to tell the police that her son "was no bad kid" before they departed. And as soon as they left, she also made a point to tell Spencer that his Silver City days were coming to an end. This incident only cemented the fears of Spencer and his mother that the big young boy's problems would only get worse if he stayed.

Considering how long Spencer wanted out, he was all ears about the plan to finally leave Mississippi.

"My mom wasn't gonna let me go down like this," Spencer said. "So we started [planning this] journey with the idea of me going to Chicago. That was my first step out."

3

A NEW HOME

SPENCER'S MOM WANTED HIM TO move up North to Chicago with his brother Joe to safely further his basketball dream and education. Considering that Spencer was ready to leave this small Mississippi town for years, he gladly accepted his mother's exit strategy. Furthermore, Spencer actually had previously spent two weeks visiting his brother in the Windy City, and loved it.

Spencer tried to get more haircutting and lawnmowing jobs to bring in the needed "little stash" for the move to Chicago. The plan was to travel with a young African American man named Leonard "Bookie" Boss who used to work as a caddy at the local golf course. Spencer said he received the nickname "Bookie" because he "used to poop in his pants when we were little." Bookie and Spencer rode up to Chicago together on a Greyhound bus.

Spencer was not lying when he said he had a "little stash" to hold him over on his trek to Chicago. He packed a big bag of food that included bologna, chicken, and white bread because he did not want to spend the little bit of money he had on food. Bookie did not have much money either.

The first stop they made on the trip to Chicago was in Memphis, Tennessee. Spencer still remembers the thrill he got hearing B.B. King's music blaring on the streets. It reminded him of his rides home from his high school coach, who always loved to play blues music. Spencer also kept his ears open for music when they made a pitstop in Nashville.

When he finally arrived in Chicago, a famished Spencer said he was sitting and eating a bologna sandwich as he waited for his brother. As he did, random Black man walked up and chastised him about eating pork, while also trying to sell him a Muslim newspaper for 15 cents, long before Minister Louis Farrakhan founded *The Final Call* newspaper in 1979. A naïve Spencer engaged with the man in debate about pork, and truly contemplated giving up some of his money for one of the newspapers. Chicago had its share of Black Muslims, who refrain from eating pork, by the time Spencer came to town in the 1960s.

"He said, 'What you eating there?'" Spencer said. "I'm like, 'I'm eating this bologna sandwich.' And he's like, 'You know you can't be eating that pork, boy.' And I was like, 'You got be crazy. This is the best bologna sandwich. My mother made it for me.' And here comes my brother Joe, saying, 'Man, don't be talking to those guys, man. Those guys are Black Muslims.'

"I don't know what a Black Muslim is. But I'm thinking this guy is pretty cool to me…. So Joe was explaining to me, 'Them people are bad people there.' And I was like, 'Yeah whatever, he seemed pretty cool to me.'"

Spencer was living in Chicago with Andrew, Lena Mae, Joe, and Lavaughn. Life was good quickly for Spencer in Chicago, primarily because he was at home on the basketball court. He had a pair of Converse to dunk in, water to quench his thirst, and he would work on his game when he was by himself. When he did play against what he described as "the city boys," he built a reputation of never getting tired while holding his own. And when he played against the family star in Leroy, a Bowling Green State University basketball standout, well Spencer would hold his own then, too.

"It was the most joyous time I've ever had.... We could play basketball all day, I didn't have to work or do nothing, so I was just balling and balling and balling," Spencer said.

Impressed with his little brother, Leroy landed him a tryout with Detroit Pershing High School basketball coach Will Robinson at Kronk Gym.

Robinson immediately took a liking to Spencer and wanted him at Pershing. Spencer accepted the life-changing offer right off, unaware that the legendary basketball coach would end up becoming a father figure to him off the court. Robinson cared about more than just basketball, and would get Spencer back on the right track academically as well. Robinson, who ended up becoming the first Black Division I basketball coach and scouted for the Detroit Pistons, helped more than 300 young men earn college basketball scholarships.

"He saw me and we were just talking about life, basketball, and education, because he was a stickler for education," Spencer said. "'We got to start off getting you reading all over again, boy, because you done fell so far behind. We got to get you a tutor.' And the tutor he got me turned out to be Dr. Wayne Dyer, who ended up becoming a famous author. He was teaching at Pershing and took me under his arm and was like, 'I got a protégé, this is my first guinea pig.'"

Robinson also found a host family for Spencer in James and Ida Bell, who lived off Seven Mile Road in Detroit in Conant Gardens. They would later legally adopt Spencer so he could attend Pershing. James was a foreman and Ida was a nurse. Spencer shared a bedroom with their son, Gregory, but he had his own bed in a house with running water, bathrooms, and a shower.

Certainly, the Bell home was much more modern than the "shanty" Spencer had lived in back home in Mississippi.

"I'm hoping that they like me and so I'm trying to sell myself," Spencer said. "And Mrs. Bell tells me, 'Baby, you don't have to sell yourself like this. We like you. You're going to be alright here. There's Gregory's bed over there, but you're going to have to have to share a room now.' And I was like, 'But I'm not gonna share a bed?' I just had a big bed and room. I'm like, *Well, shit.... I came out of a three-room shanty, and now I'm living here? A toilet? Big showers?"*

Mrs. Bell noticed that Spencer walked around slumping with a lack of confidence. That came from all those years in Mississippi of being told he was nothing, being told he was a "nigger." So she worked with him on his posture and proper etiquette. There was also Dr. Dyer, whose focus was self-development, and he helped a great deal as well.

"I had to walk around with a book on my head because Mrs. Bell wanted me to not be embarrassing," Spencer said. "I didn't know all of that stuff, I was kind of a doofus. I was dragging because I had been beat down in Mississippi. So, everything I got, when I was getting ready to eat, it was everything with a spoon. I had to set up my fork with my left hand, which I didn't want to do. But I had to learn how to do it to use the knife with my right hand. They taught me etiquette. They taught me posture too, her and Dr. Dyer."

Robinson, Dyer, and the Bells, however, could not protect Spencer from getting laughed at by the students when he showed up with his minimal Mississippi wardrobe and country twang. He had two pair of raggedy well-worn jeans, one pair of corduroy pants, and some gifted Chuck Taylors. Spencer also let you know where he was from immediately with his Mississippi accent. Keep in mind this was before they knew anything about him as a basketball player. The first two weeks of school were rough for Spencer, and the for the first time he did not feel welcomed.

"When I came into Pershing High School that first day they let me have it," Spencer said. "They were like, 'This guy here. Where is he coming from? This country nigga. Oh God, there's a country nigga in the house.' So, I was like *Oh boy*. I didn't know their families had just came up too. I was gullible. They were just putting me down. And I was drawling with my accent, 'What do y'all want?'

"The first two weeks I was kind of beat down. I was slumped down. But I was like, *Wait until the season comes. Y'all gone like me.* But in the meanwhile, I got to go through this shit."

Ida Bell eventually got wind of what Spencer was going through and took him to a clothing store called Hot Sam's Detroit. This men's fashion store in Downtown Detroit was opened in 1921 and is still open today. Mrs. Bell bought Spencer some sweaters, wingtip shoes, and other clothes. But Mrs. Bell was also a little out of touch with the current culture, which innocently led to more teasing for the new student.

"We were all getting ready for that first game and I wanted the alligator shirt, a sweater, and a polo shirt," Spencer said. "She didn't buy me that alligator shirt. But she got me one that looked like it and

I had my wingtip shoes. And I thought I was going to be a star at this high school. And of course, when I got there they laughed at me."

While the kids were teasing the country kid from Mississippi, he was learning much more than he did in his home state. While Spencer had a lot of making up to do for his age, he was taking quality English and math classes. He wrote his first name with a lower case "s" when he was asked as a new student to write his name on the chalkboard. His teacher quickly corrected that. Spencer said he had an English teacher named Mrs. Sommerville, who spent extra time with him after class to help him get up to speed. Spencer went from a horrible student to owning a respectable B-average with all the help.

Looking back, Spencer credited Robinson for all the life-altering help.

"All of a sudden I had my English classes, math classes, and all this stuff," Spencer said. "I was so far behind at the time…. Because in Mississippi the idea of the school was not to educate me.

"When it was cotton-picking time and wood-chopping time, the schools closed down. If they educated me, I would leave the farm because I was being an educated nigga and that was just a no-no. So then I had to start all over."

You know the old saying that it takes a village to raise a child? Well, it truly took a village in Detroit to change Spencer from a country boy from Mississippi with a Southern drawl to an educated city kid. And these folks aiding Spencer were all connected to Robinson.

Along with the Bell family and Dr. Dyer, Mrs. Sommerville was very important as well. Spencer said that she considered him "an important project to her." She took time after school to help him catch up academically. He also got tutoring in mathematics. Spencer's basketball potential surely played a major role, but these adults worked hard to develop Spencer.

"Everybody else was like, 'Well we don't want a dummy. We want strong representation,'" Spencer said.

There are 907 miles between Silver City and Detroit, for an estimated 14-hour drive today. Yes, Spencer missed his beloved mama in his first departure from the home he knew. But his disgust for the racist life in Mississippi kept him from being homesick. A whole new fair world for an American Negro in Michigan was mentally stimulating, educational, fresh, and easy to fall in love with.

While Spencer was finally alive in Detroit, he did not forget where he came from and still reached out to his supportive and spiritual mother regularly. To get ahold of his mother, who did not have a home phone, he would have to call Alexander Grocery Store in Silver City. Spencer's mother would also talk to Mrs. Bell every week to get an update from an adult and a female.

"She was this spiritual lady," Spencer said. "She would say, 'The Lord's got you in the right place. He has you where I have wanted you to be for all of these years and you are on your way.'"

Mrs. Bell was truly Spencer's mother away from home, with her daily love, support, and constructive criticism. She even wore the same red dress to every one of Spencer's games at Detroit Pershing High so he could pick her out in the stands easily. And once Spencer was playing well and Pershing High became aware of the lady in red in the stands, the fans viewed her as a good luck charm.

"She wore it no matter how big the venue was that we were playing in," Spencer said. "She wore it to every game. And when she wore that red dress, after the first game when I turned that shit out, they told her, 'Please, wear the red dress.' And so, she never missed a game."

Spencer lived up to the hype from the start as a basketball player at Detroit Pershing High, just like he had back at McNair, and quickly gained popularity in the process. He joined forces with guard Ralph Simpson, who was the son of a Harlem Globetrotter and would later become an American Basketball Association star (and the father of R&B singer India Arie). The Spencer-Simpson duo led Detroit Pershing High School to a 1967 Michigan state championship.

Spencer said a predominately Black public school winning a state championship was rare because of racism from White referees.

"A Detroit city public school hadn't won the state championship in 35 years," Spencer said. "It was a drought, because once you get out of the city, the whistle is blown a different way. [Robinson] got a great guard because I needed somebody to help me with this shit. So, he moved Ralph Simpson from over at Southeastern into the Pershing district. So his father, who played with the 'Trotters, Will knew really well, and now we had a one-two punch."

After winning a state championship, Spencer said he had a beautiful, "real cool prom date." He actually got a Michigan driver's license and borrowed a Thunderbird drop-top car from a friend named Leroy for the fancy event. Spencer said he did not have sexual intercourse with his prom date and graduated high school still a virgin. His sexual status quickly changed once he went on a recruiting trip to the University of Tennessee, where he had relations with a young Black female student.

"I did walk across that stage as a virgin," Spencer said. "Will Robinson had a block on me. He was like, 'The one thing that is going to mess you up is girls.'"

Spencer was recruited hard by the University of Michigan and the University of Tennessee, but he said that Robinson blocked him from going to Michigan because of how they wrongly treated one of his former players. Haywood was not open to going back home to play for Ole Miss or Mississippi State due to the racism in his old state.

Tennessee seemed to be the right choice for Spencer. He would have been the first Black player in Southeastern Conference history. But Spencer said that racism from legendary Kentucky basketball coach Adolph Rupp ultimately ended up being the reason Spencer did not play for Tennessee either, after a tenuous phone conversation.

"I was gonna be the first brother in the SEC and then here comes Adolph Rupp and that whole Kentucky thing," Spencer said. "They had just lost to Texas Western, so they had some kind of contract in the Southeastern Conference that they were going to get the first Black player. When I talked to him on the phone it reminded me of Silver City, Mississippi.

"He was a nice man, but I was scared of him. He was like, 'The one thing you can't do when you come down here, you can't date no White girls.' I didn't really know about dating White girls, but I was like, *I would like to have the option because I'm a student.* Then the University of Tennessee gets shaky legs because the big boys are calling and want to control that conference."

For a moment, just consider what Spencer could have meant to Michigan or the history of the SEC if he had played for Tennessee, Ole Miss, or Mississippi State.

Spencer said that Robinson told him to "abandon ship" and put him on a plane from Knoxville, Tennessee, to Denver. Coach told Spencer that he had a junior college that he should play for called Trinidad State Junior College in Trinidad, Colorado. Spencer said that Robinson sold him on the school by saying that it was in-between Denver and Albuquerque.

But by the time Spencer and his buddy Wiley finished the long drive from metropolitan Denver to rural Trinidad, he realized he was in the middle of nowhere. Trinidad was also known for being a gun-manufacturing town.

More importantly though, some good Black ballplayers were there, as integration in major college basketball was still a work in progress.

"We go to lunch in the lunchroom and we're looking at the team and we had some brothers—mainly brothers. We had some White boys, too," Spencer said. "So, I was like, *Oh shit, we're gonna ball.* Back then in '67 and '68, a lot of the bad dudes were in junior college because they had just started accepting Black guys into Division I. So all of the bad dudes—Cliff Meely, Johnny Johnson—they were all in our conference.

"So we start balling man, and I start jumping out of the gym, feeling great, just balling. That was a good time, Trinidad."

Spencer definitely had a good time in Trinidad on the court during the 1967–68 season, as he averaged a dominant 28.2 points and 22.1 rebounds per game. He also enjoyed taking the team bus around the Rocky Mountain Region playing basketball games and seeing the beauty of that part of the country.

"The school was very nice, man," Spencer said. "The food was good because you were in cattle country. We had a nice lunchroom, but the road trips were just the shit because we were getting all of those big sirloin steaks, Porterhouses."

Spencer expected to be a one-and-done at Trinidad by accepting a full basketball scholarship to the University of New Mexico.

"That was the whole trail," Spencer said, "Trinidad to New Mexico."

That was the plan, at least.

4

USA BASKETBALL

SPENCER'S STELLAR PLAY NOT ONLY had bigger colleges looking, it got him noticed by USA Basketball. Keep in mind, this is 1968, and 34 years before the arrival of the Dream Team, with Michael Jordan, Magic Johnson, Larry Bird, and other NBA stars. Some of the best amateurs at this time—most notably UCLA star Lew Alcindor, who would later change his name to Kareem Abdul-Jabbar—boycotted the '68 Olympics, declining to play for the USA in the final years of the Civil Rights Movement to protest the poor treatment of Blacks in America.

Spencer, however, accepted an invite to try out for the 1968 USA Basketball Olympic team with other junior-college players. He said that Robinson successfully campaigned to get him the invite. Spencer was more interested in wearing red, white, and blue for his country than boycotting, since he really was not very educated about the Olympics anyway, being from rural Mississippi.

"I didn't know much about the stance by Black athletes at the time," Spencer said. "But I knew about the picture that Kareem, Jim Brown, and everybody did. And I saw where Martin Luther King was saying,

'I'm not going to expect anything from the players; I would like to see them not boycott.' But if the Americans boycott, is it the proper thing to do? So, I didn't know, then all of a sudden, Will [Robinson] is calling the coach because he is orchestrating this shit.

"I didn't even know what the Olympics were. I was just balling, man. I hadn't seen the 1964 Olympics—I didn't know anything about that shit. I'd just read about it in magazines."

Spencer said that famed college basketball coach Jerry Tarkanian, who would later lead the University of Nevada Las Vegas, stated publicly that in the late 1960s junior colleges were producing better basketball players than Division I. Robinson also sold Spencer on the fact that he was as good—and potentially better—than anyone trying out for USA Basketball team.

Robinson instilled confidence that Robinson would make the cut and would be an elite member. Spencer was skeptical, since he was only 19 years old, and was most interested in just getting as much USA Basketball gear as possible before he got cut. Spencer said he tried out and made the team after playing well in tryouts in Albuquerque. And in the end, Robinson ended up being correct as a shocked Spencer was selected.

"They said the first player picked was me," Spencer said. "I was still looking around like, *What are they talking about?* Because honestly, I came down there for the bags and the gear. Well, I thought I could make the team, but they kept telling me I was too young. They wanted experience.

"So, my thoughts were, *I can at least say, 'I tried out for the team,' and I could tell those boys back in Detroit I got a US Olympic bag.* I got those warmups and they were some sweet warmups. I got some pretty good-looking shit that says "USA." Now, all of a sudden I'm a citizen. I had a moment; I was ecstatic. I didn't believe it, but I believed it."

Spencer called his mother to tell her the good news. She could not have been prouder. He started thinking about how amazing it would be for his lovers and haters in Silver City, Mississippi, and his friends from Detroit, to see him on television playing for the United States in the Olympics. Even if you were racist in Silver City, it was inevitable that you would feel pride when one of your own from your tiny town made it to the Olympics.

Spencer's confidence was growing dramatically, and he felt that he was the best player on a roster that included stellar Kansas guard Jo Jo White and North Carolina star forward Charlie Scott. Unfortunately, there was one big potential roadblock for Spencer. He did not have a birth certificate to prove his United States nationality and his age.

"I just thought I was the shit," Spencer said. "I didn't care if it was Kareem or whoever, I was kicking his ass. That's where I was. It was gravy. When we played in Alamosa, [USA coach] Hank Iba was like, 'This is the guy that's going to do it.' He was telling me this, pumping me up, and then Jo Jo and Charlie were running their mouth saying, 'We can win this shit and win the gold medal.'

"All of a sudden the big question came up for me: 'Where is your birth certificate so we can go and get your passport?' I didn't have a birth certificate. I was the only one on the team who didn't have a birth certificate, so there was a panic going on."

Spencer's mother still did not have a phone in 1968, so USA Basketball called the Alexander Grocery Store in Silver City, Mississippi, to get ahold of her for a proof of birth for her son. She quickly departed in search of a birth certificate, which she ended up finding in a Silver City kind of way.

Spencer Haywood's name was written in a Holy Bible when he was born. Well, actually, the first name "Spensie" and his birthdate were written in one of his mother's Bibles. After checking it out to make sure it was authentic, USA Basketball was able to get the Bible to pass as a proof of birth for "Spensie." Well, Spencer.

And to Spencer's extreme delight, after coming from the cotton fields and being seen as "subhuman," he actually owned a United States of America passport.

"It was written in the Bible," Spencer said. "They had to go take a picture of the Bible. I was born April 22. They took the picture, took it down to Jackson, got the birth certificate, and low and behold my name is spelled 'Spensie,' and everybody knows me as Spencer. So they had to make that correction.

"But when I got that passport it was… *beyond*, like a dream in America. I was picking cotton. I was subhuman. I was like nothing. And now I have a passport and I'm going overseas to represent the United States."

Haywood's passport got put to good use immediately, as USA Basketball played exhibition games in Russia, Yugoslavia, and Finland. Team USA was coached by a White man in Henry Iba, whose staff included a Black pioneer coach with a brilliant offensive mind in John McLendon. Spencer said that Iba and McLendon also told the Black players to stay away from White women.

But when Spencer got to Finland, the kid from Mississippi disobeyed his coaches when he had his first opportunity to be intimate with a White woman.

"The White women over there in Finland were looking at us Black men like we were Gods," Spencer said. "I didn't get none until just before we were leaving, because Hank Iba and John McLendon were not having it. So, I snuck me a piece because I wanted to tap me a White girl. I never had one."

USA Basketball next went to New York City, where they played in an exhibition game on September 28, 1968, against the New York Knicks. Spencer would be matched up against one of the NBA's top big men in Willis Reed. Spencer said he got the better of Reed as USA won the exhibition aired on ABC.

After the notable USA win, legendary American sportscaster Howard Cosell interviewed Spencer.

"I kicked Willis Reed's ass good. We won, too," Spencer said. "And that's when Howard Cosell got on the bandwagon, because he was doing his ABC broadcast, 'Well, I think we got one here.' He started rambling about this young phenom—me. I didn't know what a 'phenom' was, but I figured it must be some cool shit.

"I knew who he was because of Muhammad Ali. But my interview was guarded, because Hank Iba and John McLendon were right next to me all in my ear. So I couldn't say too much, just, 'Yes sir,' or 'No sir.' And, 'I just want to bring back the gold for the United States, and that's all I ever wanted in life.' Blah, blah, blah. I was kind of prepped for it."

Next up for USA was another exhibition, this time against NBA superstar Oscar Robertson and the Cincinnati Royals. Spencer was very excited for this match-up since he was playing against his favorite player in "The Big O." Even so, Spencer was not intimidated as he tried to block every signature one-handed shot that Robertson tossed up.

By the end of the match, Robertson had respect for Spencer and Team USA.

"We go to Cincinnati to play the Cincinnati Royals and my favorite player, 'The Big O,'" Spencer said. "'The Big O' was shooting that sweet shot. I started jumping over our guards and blocking his shit. And that's when O said to me, 'Y'all gonna win this shit [the Olympics].' When he said that I almost pissed all over myself.

"He came from the same background as me. He was a farm boy in Indiana. And Will Robinson used to tell me, 'He ain't nothing but a big ol' farm boy, just like you.' But he's the best in the world."

Next up on Spencer's passport was Mexico City for the 1968 Olympics. While Spencer arrived confident and focused on winning a gold medal, little did he know that he was going to witness a notable moment in Black history in the process and the aftermath that came with it.

Spencer and the USA Olympic team arrived in Mexico on the heels of something that would hit home to a lot of the young athletes. Ten days before the start of the Olympics, there were peaceful student protests taking place that turned deadly.

On October 2, 1968, Mexican students gathered to protest for democratic and civil rights at the Plaza de las Tres Culturas, a public square in Mexico City. Students were also unhappy that the Mexican government had spent $175 million on the 1968 Olympics, which would be more than $1 billion today. The students chanted, "¡No queremos olimpiadas, queremos revolución!" which translates to, "We don't want Olympics, we want revolution!" The students also gave speeches to express their thoughts.

The Mexican government ordercd that the student protests be broken up. Over 500 Mexican Army soldiers with 200 tanks showed up and responded by killing hundreds of protestors and civilians and arresting over 1,000 people. The Mexican national media wrongly portrayed it as a violent student protest at that time, which made it believed internationally that the military response was just. It was later revealed that the student protest was peaceful upon the military's arrival. The unforgettable Mexican tragedy is now known as The Tlatelolco Massacre.

"We flew into Mexico City and they had the student riots," Spencer said. "There were about eight or nine kids that had been killed on campus, so as we are arriving they are sweeping up blood off the street. We are on the bus like, 'They're trying to make this shit look really good for the Olympics.'"

There was a lot to see at the Olympics for Spencer when he had down time. Beautiful venues. Beautiful women from all over the world. But for a kid from Mississippi who often had to hunt for his food, no place was better than the cafeteria at the Olympic Village. The cafeteria included all-you-can-eat food from all over the world 24 hours per day.

And Spencer certainly made his presence known with a plate and fork there, just as well as he did on the basketball court.

"We get over to that village man—they had built this beautiful village and had all of this food," Spencer said. "We went in there and [USA Basketball teammate] Charlie Scott was on my head saying, 'Boy, you are country.' They said that because I was looking for food. I was always looking for food.

"You have to remember, [Scott and Jo Jo White] were used to shit, going to schools like North Carolina and Kansas. I was the goofball hanging out with the big boys. I was looking at one thing. I wasn't looking at women, I wasn't looking at nothing but food. I couldn't get enough; I was growing."

It was there that Spencer met a new friend, a man who would become one of the greatest boxers of all-time: George Foreman.

Foreman won the gold medal in the heavyweight division in boxing at the 1968 Mexico City Olympic Games. The Houston native defeated the Soviet Union's Jonas Čepulis after the referee stopped the fight in the second round. Foreman walked around the ring carrying a small American flag and bowing to the crowd after winning the bout to the ire of his fellow African Americans back home fighting for Civil Rights and hoping for change.

"George, I hadn't seen him fight or anything, but I heard everybody talking about him," Spencer said. "George put them Russians to sleep. The world was all about the Russians. George said when he knocked the Russian out he was going to wave the American flag. George had just come out of poverty, he didn't have a place to stay either.

"People were calling him an Uncle Tom. But I wasn't. Hell no. That was my eating partner. Not only that, but we were two young guys who were there for our country who wanted to move up in life."

Collectively, Spencer and Foreman also knocked out a lot of food while enjoying each other's company. While known for their personalities now, Spencer said both were shy Southern boys at the time who bonded in the cafeteria with hungry athletes from around the world.

"He was always in that lunch room, too," Foreman said. "Between me, George, the Russians, all of the Eastern Bloc countries, the

Africans, we were just in there eating all of the time. We didn't have to leave from too far away because we were close to the lounge. After we ate, we would go relax and let it dissolve a little bit, then go back and get some more. It was beautiful, man.

"They had all kinds of food because they had the world's food, everybody was there. I was strictly with the American food though; I didn't want to do any experimenting. Hamburgers, hot dogs, steaks—I loved the meat because I didn't have any as a kid."

Another American Olympic star that Spencer met in the cafeteria at the Olympic Village was three-time gold medalist sprinter Wilma Rudolph. Rudolph, then 28 years old, was not competing anymore but was attending as a U.S. ambassador. Like Spencer, she hailed from the South. She was born in Saint Bethlehem, Tennessee, and grew up in Clarksville, Tennessee.

Spencer was excited to see a sistah from the South, and had a crush on the beautiful 5-foot-11 woman. Rudolph passed away at the young age of 54 in 1994 after a bout with brain and throat cancer.

"I was like, *Oh my God, look at this lady*," Spencer said. "She had the beautiful legs, beautiful skin. She was a sprinter. She won bronze in 1956, and in 1960 became the first woman to win three golds in track-and-field. We started talking about where we were from. She went to Tennessee State University, so she was really cool."

Perhaps part of the reason why Spencer was eating so much was he was actually extremely nervous about playing in the Olympics.

Spencer was overwhelmed by the media attention he was getting from the American journalists, most notably Cosell. USA had won all six gold medals in the Olympic men's basketball competitions they had competed in. Spencer also had never played basketball on such a high level before. Noticing the teenager was nervous, Robinson flew from Detroit to Mexico City to calm him down.

"Will Robinson came down because I was getting nervous the closer we got to the games," Haywood said. "I realized it was a big deal. Before it was like, 'So what?' But now Cosell and everybody was talking about, 'If they lose, it's going to be your fault.' I'm starting to feel the pressure; I'm stressed."

Spencer said that Robinson thought some mature female companionship would relax him. So Robinson introduced him to an American track star named Willye White. She was a two-time silver medalist who competed in five Olympics and, as it turned out, was from Greenwood, Mississippi, only about 15 miles from where Spencer was from. White, who passed away in 2007 at age 67, was nine years older than a then-19-year-old Spencer when he said they had a relationship in Mexico City.

"I was starting to feel the pressure," Spencer said. "I'm stressed. I called Will Robinson and told him I was stressed and he comes down and somehow he knew the woman who was in the cafeteria with us and was like, 'That's who you need to be with. That's your girl.' I was like, 'That's a real woman.' He was like, 'That's somebody to look out for you.'

"I was dating her on campus and now I have support around me. I have her. Will Robinson approved of her because she was older. I remember when we was making love, she was an athlete and I was like, 'Wow.'"

5

THE 1968 OLYMPICS

THE OPENING CEREMONY OF THE 1968 Summer Olympic Games was held at the Estadio Olímpico Universitario in Mexico City. It was the start of the first Olympics ever to be held in Latin America. Mexican track-and-field athlete Enriqueta Basilio was the last torchbearer and lit the Olympic Cauldron, becoming the first woman to ever do so.

Spencer recalls African athletes wearing colorful clothes during the Opening Ceremony, Mexicans wearing sombreros, and Europeans dressed to the nines. But the Mississippi kid thought USA looked great too. It was also the first time Spencer noticed the biggest stars of the USA Olympic team: Tommie Smith, John Carlos, and Lee Evans.

"We had on our jackets, our slacks. I was sharp," Spencer said. "When you are walking into that stadium that place is going nuts. You hear them say 'United States' and you perk up. Then I'm looking up in the front and see that we have to follow the track guys—Tommie Smith, John Carlos, Lee Evans—the track team. We had kind of established ourselves before we got there so we were hot shit too, kind of like the focal point. So I was feeling like I was kind of up there with Tommie and John."

Smith and Carlos were also quietly working on a protest behind the scenes if they were on the medal stand as winners in the 200 Meters. Spencer said that the USA Olympic committee had legendary track star Jesse Owens speak to the athletes before the 1968 Olympic Games. Owens won four gold medals in the 1936 Berlin Olympics in front of Adolph Hitler, thus crushing Hitler's hopes of using the Games to demonstrate Aryan superiority.

Despite his victory over Hitler, Owens preached to the athletes not to protest, according to Spencer, with the African Americans in mind. With all due to respect to Owens, John Carlos vocalized his disdain for that mind-frame, to the surprise of Spencer.

"Jesse was telling us not to protest, speaking primarily to the Black athletes," Spencer said. "When he walked in that door we knew it was some important shit. He was a little bit 'Uncle Tom-ish,' but he was explaining how we had to get jobs when we got back and John tells him, 'We ain't gonna get shit!' I was sitting like, 'Wow, he said that to Jesse Owens.' Tommie's like me, he's country. But John isn't.

"It was interesting, because how could he say something to Jesse Owens, man? But you knew where John was coming from. He had some balls, man—some bull balls. Wilma Rudolph was mad at John. She was in his ear going off and I was like, *Whoa, I ain't gonna do nothing.*"

Spencer said that there was some fear behind the scenes from USA Basketball that Smith and Carlos were revolutionaries who could fire up Black athletes. Spencer and his Black teammates were warned by his Black and White coaches—and even their coaches back home—not to do anything political during the Olympics.

"I didn't get a chance to know those guys at the time," Spencer said. "I just knew they were some people that we were supposed to stay away from. Will Robinson was like, 'Those boys are revolutionaries, and I don't want you getting no Goddamn ideas.' [North Carolina men's basketball coach] Dean Smith was all in Charlie's ear telling him not to mess up. Same thing with the coach at Kansas with Jo Jo.

"They didn't tell us to stay away from Tommie and John. They just said to be careful. They were with the track guys. And we knew it was going to be something, we just didn't know what."

"The Star-Spangled Banner" blared through the speakers of the packed stadium when USA's Olympic team walked into Estadio Olímpico Universitario. Hearing the American national anthem conjured mixed emotions for Spencer because of his sad beginnings, which evoked thoughts of slavery. It also brought him to tears.

"It was different for me hearing it because I came from slavery," Spencer said. "I know people are going to say I wasn't a slave, but I was. I came from being an indentured servant. In three years' time, I had gone from picking and chopping cotton as a slave to being a hero for the United States.

"So, I'm crying during the Opening Ceremony. I got on an American uniform. As a family, my mother was big on America. She would send her boys to the Army. My brother Joe was in the war. The rest of us were in college or too tall, it didn't get any better than this. Very emotional, then the competition began."

Racism back in America did not dissuade Spencer from playing for the United States, but as referenced earlier, it did keep college basketball's biggest star at the time, UCLA center Lew Alcindor (who would change his name soon after to Kareem Abdul-Jabbar) from wearing the Red, White, and Blue. With all due respect to Spencer or anyone else playing for USA Basketball, none came close to being as good as Alcindor.

Alcindor led the Bruins to a national championship under legendary coach John Wooden in each of his three years from 1967 to '69. The 7-foot-2 center respectfully boycotted the Olympics to protest what he believed was injustices against African Americans. Alcindor's preference was to instead use his platform to be a social justice voice for Black people. Before going on to become the NBA's all-time leading scorer and playing alongside Magic Johnson with the Los Angeles Lakers, Alcindor received criticism, racial epithets, and death threats for his decision not to play in the Olympics. There were also several other standout college basketball players who skipped the Olympics for various reasons, but none bigger than Alcindor.

Without Alcindor, Spencer believed the Black players on USA's basketball team were viewed poorly by the Black community back in the States. But Spencer added that no one tried to convince him not to play, because they had no clue who he was and how good he was as the only player on the roster from a junior college.

"I thought his stance was commendable," Spencer said. "Elvin Hayes and Wes Unseld signing their pro contracts also opened the doors for me. No, I didn't think about the Civil Rights Movement at the time. I just wanted a passport....

"The Black players on our team were looked at as Uncle Toms for going to the Olympics. We were sellouts."

So instead of Alcindor, USA was led by White, Scott, and this diamond-in-the-rough Mississippi kid in Spencer. Without Alcindor, USA Basketball wasn't even the favorite entering the Olympics.

Yugoslavia and the Soviet Union actually defeated the Americans in two of out of three exhibition games played, respectively, prior to the Olympics in Europe. White and forward Bill Hosket and USA Basketball coach Henry Iba, however, did not take part in those exhibitions.

The social challenge was bigger for Spencer than basketball. His Olympic experience exposed him to something he had never before encountered: a substantive relationship with a White person. Considering Spencer's background, the Mississippi upbringing, the segregation of Detroit, and the way basketball consumed him, Spencer had not associated with too many White people prior to his trip to Mexico City.

Spencer roomed with a White teammate named Bill Hosket, a two-time All-Big Ten forward from Ohio State University.

"It was cool because he was from the Big Ten, Ohio State, and they paired us together because we were the centers and forwards," he said. "He was from the Midwest and it fit what they were trying to do with the Olympic Team. And he taught me so much in that span of time because I had never experienced that. After two weeks, I felt right at home. I felt very protected by him because he was a senior.

"It was strange. Because if I slept near a White person in Mississippi, they would have killed my ass. It was a little strange, but that's the beauty of sports. Sports just transcends everything because the idea is that you want to win. Here we are, all the protest that was going on, all the Black and White issues that was going on, and then you've got me rooming with a White guy! And I'm supposed to save America.

"I was like, *I'm happy in here. I've got a big ol' room.* I told him what I was going through down South."

Hosket shared an adoration of basketball with Spencer and that is want bonded them. They spent many scorching Mexico City nights talking basketball. Basketball is want brought them together, it's the reason why they were in the midst of eventful and improbable journeys. (Hosket would play four seasons in the NBA, eventually winning an NBA title with the 1970 New York Knicks as a backup forward.)

Spencer then would go down to the activity room in the hotel and attempt to play cards with Jo Jo White, Charlie Scott, Calvin Fowler, and Jim King, and they would rebuff his efforts to play, telling him to go back and hang with the "White boy."

His education continued.

The Americans opened their Olympic play with a blowout 81–46 preliminary round victory over the Spanish. Spencer first made his presence known by scoring a team-high 16 points during a preliminary round 93–36 rout over Senegal. Spencer said the Black USA players were very excited about playing the African country because they assumed they were good at basketball too, because they were Black. Spencer added that some of the White players made what he viewed as an innocent racist comment toward the Senegalese players as well.

"We stomped a hole into them," Spencer said. "I do remember us playing Senegal, because for some reason we weren't scared of the White boys, but when it came to the Africans we looked at them different, because they looked like us so we assumed they could play like us. We didn't want to take them lightly, we were going to put a boot on these guys.

"The White guys on our team got personal with the Senegalese, saying, 'We're stomping these guys back to Africa.' We knew they didn't mean anything harmful by it, because when we beat the Russians we would say, 'We're stomping them back to Russia.'"

While Spencer selfishly and naïvely didn't take the racist comments toward the Senegalese players from his White USA teammates personal, he said that White and Scott did. In fact, Spencer said Scott and White teammate Mike Barrett got into a scuffle in the locker room after the Senegal triumph.

"I didn't give a shit. Charlie and Jo Jo and some of the other guys felt a way," Spencer said. "But me I was like, 'I'm doing this for America. For myself. My country. I'm getting my mother out of this cotton field. I'm not a sellout, I'm an American—I got a passport.' So, when we had to play against the African countries it got a little tense because of the circumstances.

"But Charlie and Mike's scuffle wasn't that bad. Hank Iba would have shot both of them on the spot. They were just arguing all up in each other's face. Before it got racial, [USA assistant coach] John McLendon stepped in and said. 'We're Americans, we do stomp on everybody.' And after that we remembered every country was our enemy and we changed our tune a little bit."

Around the same time of that quiet racial incident, there was another racially charged moment that made a worldwide statement on October 16, 1968, when John Carlos and Tommie Smith offered a Black power salute to the world.

Smith finished with the gold medal in the men's 200-meter race, Australian Peter Norman finished second and Carlos finished third. While on the medal podium, as "The Star-Spangled Banner" blared in the Olympic Stadium in Mexico City, Smith and Carlos bowed their heads down and each raised a fist with a Black glove to the sky. All three medalists also wore human-rights badges on their jackets.

While the entire world bared witness to this Black power salute, a stunned Spencer was watching it on television at the Olympic Village.

"My reaction to them being on the podium was, 'What the hell?'" Spencer said. "I was in the lounge eating by myself, but other people were around in the lounge. So I'm looking at that and saying to myself, 'These guys came down here, won this shit for this country, and do this?' Now everybody is coming to our dorms and telling us, 'Don't you think of doing no shit like that.' Making sure we didn't do anything like that because we were the next big attraction. You had track, then basketball, then boxing.

"Then Hank Iba had been drinking some gin and is all concerned and shit. And Will told me, 'If you even think of trying it, I'm going to kill you. You won't even get back to Detroit. I'm going to kill you right here.'"

Spencer did not truly understand the impact of what Smith and Carlos had done until he saw them being rushed into the Olympic Village to get their belongings before being sent home. Spencer was stunned, describing how Smith and Carlos got treated as "horrible"— and this was by United States of America officials after winning medals for their country. Spencer also remembers president of the International Olympic Committee Avery Brundage screaming at Smith and Carlos.

"I remember the aftermath, and when they came to get their stuff out of the dorm they had all of this security," Spencer said. "I didn't see the big deal of them just putting the glove up. It didn't register to me that they had done something so Earth shattering. But everybody—the Olympic committee, the broadcasters—were just going crazy and shook up about this thing. And here these guys are, moving out after they won the shit, and everybody is treating them like shit.

"We were in the same area because we were the male athletes. It was so horrible. They were being treated like pieces of shit. It was so horrible—and it reminded me so much of when I was 13 and 14 in Mississippi. It was the same shit."

Suddenly, Spencer's naïveté was gone. While this Olympic stardom, passport, and free food was mind blowing for this young Black man, his mind raced back to when he and his family picked cotton in Mississippi. He recalled that nothing his family did was good enough for their White cotton-farm owners.

And Spencer realized that winning medals was not bigger than civil or human rights, and ultimately he was going to still return home as a Black man.

"I just felt so bad for them," Spencer said. "It wasn't supposed to be that big of a deal. I was young. I didn't know that it was gonna be that big of a deal. To me, it just seemed like these guys didn't boycott, came and performed for America, did their deed, did all of that training up in the mountains before the Olympics, and then they do it for America, pushing us over the top in the medal race. We're all looking over as a team trying to win medals and see how many we have.

"This was a team sport—it's not just track and basketball and shit like that—we're trying to beat the medal count. That was the whole purpose of the U.S. *team*. So seeing that—how they were treated—that was a big blow to me. And the way Avery Brundage was behaving—he was behaving like a Nazi. Then I find out later that he was. [Brundage fought against the U.S. boycott of the 1936 Olympics in Berlin, refused to cancel the 1972 Munich Games when 11 Israeli athletes were killed by Palestinian terrorists, and eventually retired to Germany after stepping down as IOC president.]

"They kicked [Smith and Carlos] out of the Olympic Village; they had to get out of there. Then they were being used as an example for the rest of us."

Meanwhile, back on the basketball court, USA showed that perhaps it should be the favorites to winning the gold medal after crushing Yugoslavia 73–58. Spencer got on a roll the next two games, scoring 27 and 26 points, respectively, to lead USA to preliminary-round blowout victories over Panama and Puerto Rico.

USA made it to the gold medal game by defeating Brazil 75–63 in the semifinals. The expected showdown between the Americans and the USSR in the gold medal game, however, did not take place, as Yugoslavia stunned the rival with a 63–62 victory. The Americans entered the gold medal game undefeated at 8–0, while Yugoslavia had only lost once to the aforementioned.

While Spencer played well, he became extremely nervous about the enormity of playing in a gold medal game viewed worldwide after Cosell put fear into him on the eve of the contest.

"Howard Cosell starts messing with me before the game," Spencer said. "The day before the game, he catches me alone and says, 'The country, the world, all of Mississippi, all of Detroit, they are counting on you. If you lose this it's going to be trouble.' He was trying to push a button, and sure enough, he pushed my button.

"Now, all of a sudden, I'm like, *Damn, this is enormous. They're showing this all across the world and I'm there in it.*"

Spencer was still extremely nervous after the tip-off for the gold medal game. In fact, he says he ran to the bathroom just before half-time to throw up while the clock was still ticking. The Americans were only up 32–29 at halftime of an intense gold medal game.

"My stomach is all messed up until the game," Spencer said. "If you watch the game, I go in for a lay-up, make it, and run straight into the bathroom while the game is going on. This was in the first half. My shit done boiled over so much because the crowd is in a frenzy and we are balling. My dumb ass, I can't go to the bench and say, 'Timeout. Let me come out.'

"I was a kid. I wasn't that old. The nerves hit me. I threw that shit up, brushed it off, had some water, and ran right back on the floor."

Spencer, however, calmed his nerves and got it going offensively, scoring eight points in a 17–0 run to give USA a commanding 49–29 lead in the second half. The Americans would never relinquish that lead, as Spencer scored a game-high 21 points to lead the Americans to gold.

"Jo Jo was making some sweet passes to me, so I got a couple of layups and sweet dunks in," Spencer said. "All of a sudden I was like, *Whoa, we won the gold, man.* I think I had 21 points, 14 rebounds, and six blocks.

"It was not that close. We won."

Spencer scored 145 points in nine games, for a 16.1 PPG average, while also setting a USA field goal percentage record of .719. Not bad for an unknown junior-college kid. He became a crowd favorite with the Mexican fans too, who cheered for the neighboring United States.

"The announcers are basically boosting me up, and the Mexican fans loved me all up and down the floor because Mexico is right there close to America. They knew they weren't going to win anything, so they were cheering for us," Spencer said.

There were three flag posts in the middle of the arena behind the court in place to represent the gold, silver, and bronze medal–winning teams during the medal ceremony. The American flag was in the middle and pulled up the highest when the gold medals were passed out. No American on USA Basketball's team may have been more emotional than Spencer.

"When I got that gold medal, man, I was crying like a damn child," Spencer said. "Everything came to this beautiful combination of, *Wow, we got the gold medal!* And I just happened to be the star. Everybody was yelling out my name and shit; my teammates were going crazy."

The 1968 Mexico City Olympics were actually the first to be televised worldwide in color. It was certainly a colorful Olympics, even without the new technology, as it was possibly the most revolutionary and well-known Games ever. Along with the iconic Black power salute from Smith and Carlos, and Basilio's moment for women, it was the first Games where athletes were drug tested, American long jumper Bob Beamon set a new world record with an 29.2-foot jump, and Spencer Haywood had his welcome party to the world.

"The closing ceremonies were nice, but we had won the gold medal and I was ready to get home," Spencer said.

Spencer went back to Detroit extremely worried that he would receive backlash from the Black community for participating in the Olympics. He feared being called a sellout, an "Uncle Tom," and being asked to leave. In actuality, the reaction was quite contrary as he returned as a gold medalist, the star of the USA Basketball team, an American hero, and a committed newcomer for the University of Detroit's team (where he had just transferred). He was even given the key to the City of Detroit.

"I was like, *Man I have to fly into Detroit and them dudes are gonna be mad at me and call me all kinds of shit*," Spencer said. "So I get to the airport, I'm coming off the plane getting my stuff, and people outside are cheering for me. It was the opposite of what I thought it was gonna be.

"I thought they were gonna be mad at me and run me over with a car. Detroit at the time was Black power and shit, but they were so proud of me and it made me feel very special. When I got back to Detroit, I got to hanging with all of the students on the campus and then I got the Black power feeling."

Meanwhile, back in Spencer's first home in Silver City, Mississippi, he went from an outcast to a revered star. The Black people were proud. Yes, even the White people were proud. Spencer's mother was being treated like a celebrity from everyone in town due to her gold medal–winning son who was watched on television, read about in the newspapers, and talked about on radio.

Silver City also wanted to celebrate Spencer's Olympic gold medal by having a parade for him. Since Spencer's hometown was too small to host, nearby Belzoni's mayor wanted to have it in his town. His mother's church also began preparations to celebrate the return of their native son.

Still understandably bitter from his past, Spencer declined the opportunity to accept the celebratory parade. Having a growing sense of Black pride post-Olympics also played a role in the emotional decision. While his mother did not try to change his mind at the time, she would tell her son years later while she was battling cancer that she was crushed personally by his decision.

That parade was bigger than him at that time. But he was too young and immature to understand how much it meant to his mother and the Blacks in Silver City. It would have been a day where Blacks would have been revered and respected for Spencer's international success instead of being just seen as a nigger.

"I didn't want those bastards to have any glory on me, so I turned it down," Spencer said. "It hurt my mother. I told them I wasn't coming, [but] my mother, the church, my city, they were all prepared and I didn't know. I was feeling my oats. I was feeling the Black power movement, so I had flipped a little bit. Before I was just this guy. But now I was in Detroit and we're listening to jazz. So, I'm like, 'I don't want those White sons of bitches to enjoy my shit.'

"But for my mother it was the biggest day of her life and I messed it up. She told me [that] later when she was dying with cancer. I asked her what was the biggest regret she had of me, and I thought it was gonna be when I got high with the Lakers, but it wasn't that. It was that day of the parade and what it meant for the family and the lineage of the family. I was sick for months after she passed because of that."

Suddenly, Spencer's mom went from celebrity to looked at with disappointment, because her superstar son was too big time to pay respects to where he was from. If Spencer had just went through with the parade, her life in Silver City would have been gold until her last breath. As tough as Spencer is, just the mere mention of this story brings regret, pain, and tears.

"She had scrubbed those floors. Picked that cotton. Did everything for those people in Mississippi and now she was going to have all of those people looking up to her because I brought that medal back home for the country," Spencer said. "She was a celebrity because of me. She could go into stores and not get called 'nigger.' They were just disappointed in my Black ass and the Black folks were even more disappointed. I was thinking I was Spencer Haywood, the superstar, so why would I wanna go and deal with you cotton-pickers? That arrogant attitude will take you some places—bad places.

"My biggest regret in sports history was disappointing my mother. I told you I was a mama's boy. I didn't know. And nobody stopped to explain it to me. And my mom didn't explain what it meant until later. Even when I would come home from college and my first year in the pros with my Cadillac and shit from Denver, everybody was kind of standoffish.

"It was a little different."

6

UNIVERSITY OF DETROIT

S PENCER REALLY DIDN'T UNDERSTAND THE significance of the achievement of helping Team USA win gold as a 19-year-old junior-college player. Still, despite coming from tiny Trinidad State in Trinidad, Colorado, Spencer knew he was one of the best players in America. There was no doubt.

And his next step was pretty simple. It was going home. After a year at Trinidad, Spencer decided to sign with the University of Detroit. Detroit was a basketball hotbed in the late 1960s, churning out prospects, including Spencer. Playing in his adopted home for what he believed would be for his old Pershing High School coach Will Robinson was a dream.

Robinson had become his second father, a mentor and guide. And while the University of Detroit hiring an African American head coach would be unprecedented, it wouldn't be so much for those who knew Robinson's bright basketball mind and ability to recruit the best local talent.

Spencer committed to Detroit on the promise by the athletic director that he would eventually play for Robinson. Spencer had grown to love Detroit and he became a local celebrity. He was a gold medalist at a time when the city was an entertainment and sports hotbed.

The Detroit Tigers were winning the World Series in the midst of the city's riots in 1968. Near the University, Motown Records was the most prominent label in the world, with Marvin Gaye, the Temptations, Diana Ross, Stevie Wonder, and Smokey Robinson all in their prime and all living in Detroit.

It was a volatile time, the heart of the Civil Rights Era, the Democratic Convention in Chicago, and riots sparking up all over major American cities. Spencer was not even 20 years old in the middle of the what was Black Camelot, a hero in a city of heroes.

But feeling royal was nothing new to Spencer. He had been told he was the chosen one, the one who would reach super stardom, support his family, buy his mother a Cadillac, since he was 10 years old.

At Pershing High School in Detroit, a basketball power and school that produced the likes of Mel Daniels, ABA All-Star Ralph Simpson, Kevin Willis, and Steve Smith, Spencer was dominating so much that word spread to the Detroit Pistons that there was a wunderkind who could play in the NBA right now.

"Dave Bing used to bring the Pistons over to our gym in high school and practice with us," Spencer said. "Because he was saying to those players, 'Man, you've got to see these young guys that can play. Let's scrimmage them.' And we would scrimmage them because Will Robinson, who was a scout for the Pistons, was my coach and [adoptive] dad.

"So we played against them, and I was like 'Ah shit! I'm just not dominating the high school scene.' Because Cazzie Russell and Bill Buntin and Oliver Darden would take me up to the University of Michigan to play with those guys all the time. Of course, there was light-weight recruiting going on, but I got a chance to play against college players. In fact, one of those [Michigan] players ended up on the Olympic team with me, John Clawson.

"I didn't have a big head about it, but I just knew that I belonged. I mean, I knew that because I dominated most of those guys. And they were geeking me up like, 'Ah man, you're the new second coming'—to Kareem, of course."

Before LeBron James, Spencer lived as the chosen one. He spent his childhood in Mississippi knowing there was something better for him. He spent his high school career being told he was destined for greatness, and that was proven by his Olympic performance, even if he didn't play at the major university and knew his road to success would likely be unprecedented and unchartered.

Spencer said the turning point for his basketball confidence and prowess occurred at an impromptu scrimmage in 1967 at the Kronk Gym, the same gym made famous by Detroit legend Thomas "the Hitman" Hearns.

"I knew I was very good, but when I scrimmaged against all those guys—[future NBA players] George Trapp, John Trapp [no relation], and John Brisker—Kronk had an outdoor court and we really had a lot of basketball being played. When I came up and played against all those guys and they were like, 'Man, I don't know if I can wear Converse, I need some Adidas shoes and I need this and it's gonna be too hot out here.'

"I was looking at it like, 'This is not hot at all, because I had came up from the South, where you picked cotton from sun up to sun down in the sun—the real sun!' I was like, 'We finna to play in a simple little game?'"

Spencer played three games in the "sweltering" heat that day. One was against high school players ("I killed them"); one against the college players, mostly from Michigan; and then the third game against NBA and ABA players with Detroit roots.

"I was like, 'Shit, this ain't like picking cotton,'" he said. "This is fun."

Spencer played in those scrimmages for six hours, a hint to his renowned perseverance during his professional career. Spencer loved to ball, and basketball was the only thing important to him. The game came easy, and his 6-foot-8, 230-pound wildly athletic frame allowed him to do things that even impressed the NBA players.

Players with Spencer's ability to run the floor, soar for layups and dunks (although dunks weren't nearly as prevalent 50 years ago), and shoot from midrange were rare. It was then that Spencer realized that he didn't want to wait until he was 22 years old, as was the standard rule for players wanting to enter the draft, to play in the NBA or ABA.

But he'd already signed to attend the University of Detroit. Of course, that was under the assumption that he'd be playing for Will Robinson. Robinson was 57 years old at the time and had paid his dues in the high school basketball circles. He was ready for the opportunity, but even in the north, even in a city that was considered accepting of Blacks and Black achievement, Robinson wouldn't get that opportunity.

"I wanted to be coached by him," Spencer said. "He had struggled through all of those years to build something and we knew we had George Gervin coming, we had Ralph Simpson coming, we had some serious players. We were getting ready to build this powerhouse in Detroit. So it was a big deal."

Spencer said he was recruited to Detroit by Michigan governor George W. Romney (father of future Republican presidential candidate Mitt) and Detroit mayor Jerome Cavanagh.

"They sold me on the idea that I should come back home because the riots had burned up the city. 'We need saviors now and you saved the Olympics, so bring your ass back home and save us,'" he said. "'We saved you, coming up from Mississippi.' So my loyalty was right there in Detroit. Of course.

"Of course, [former Detroit player] Dave DeBusschere did a pretty good job of recruiting me."

DeBusschere had played seven years with the Detroit Pistons, a Detroit native who'd led the University of Detroit to the NCAA Tournament. While with the Pistons, he would take high schooler Spencer to UD games.

With Russell and Buntin making a serious pitch for Spencer to attend Michigan, he was undecided until Robinson took over the decision.

"I didn't know Will Robinson had such a hard on for me not going to Michigan, because I kind of wanted to go to Michigan," he said.

But Robinson told him about his former Pershing point guard, Willie Iverson, who had to settle for Central Michigan after being rejected by Michigan. Robinson did not want to send any of his players to play for the Wolverines.

"I was like 'Man, what's that got to do with me?'" Spencer said he told Robinson. "'I'm in 1967, that was '63.' But no, he wanted that Detroit job. He had this big, drawn-out plan—long range by my senior year—we would have had George Gervin, we would have had

Ralph Simpson, George Trapp, we would have had them all. It was going to be a dynasty."

Spencer played 24 games for UD as a freshman, averaging an amazing 32.1 points per game and 22.1 rebounds as the Titans went 16–10.

Spencer considered Detroit home. He resented Mississippi. It had done nothing for him, only fostering his hatred for the subservient treatment and what he perceived as the way certain Black people accepted the oppression. He wanted to forget his upbringing. He even wanted to forget his family in certain cases.

"I didn't want to know those people," he said. "I didn't even want to know my brother Floyd, with his bad self. I didn't want to know those cotton-pickers. I'm in Detroit."

The Titans sold out most of their games at Calihan Hall (then known as the Memorial Building), the 10,000-seat arena that actually housed the Pistons for a portion of the 1950s.

Spencer said Motown artists such as Smokey Robinson would head to the corner of Fairfield and Grove to catch Spencer, Larry Moore, Dwight Dunlap, Wiley Davis, Vernell DeSilva, and Jim Jackson.

Detroit was the only Division I basketball program in the city. Michigan was in Ann Arbor, 43 miles from the city. Michigan State was 90 miles away in East Lansing.

"They came to all of the games because it was the hot thing in town," he said.

Many of those Motown artists were not much older than Spencer, so he struck up close friendships with several notable legends, including bass singer Melvin Franklin of The Temptations.

"He would sometimes come over to the practice," Spencer said. "He would be like, 'Man, let's go over to Motown,' and I would be like, 'Oh shit, we're going to Motown!' So we'd go over there and listen to the music and listen to how they would all put it together and listen to [Temptations lead singer] David Ruffin. Boy, there was something about him.

"I was like, 'How come I feel so close to this brother? What's going on here?' I didn't know it at the time, but he was a Mississippi man."

Like Spencer, Ruffin moved from small-town Mississippi to Detroit in his late teens, where he would eventually become a member of The Temptations.

"I didn't know it at the time, I just loved his singing," he said. "Detroit was such an incredible place at that time. I mean, Berry Gordy, Diana Ross, all these people coming in and out their studio and they were part of the neighborhood. We took it for granted, but it was like I had this rich life in Mississippi with all these tobacco-chewing bastards playing blues in the backwoods and we just sit there all day long. I got all that richness, all that good culture, and then I got to Detroit—the music scene, people were rich—Black and White—the auto industry was moving."

Spencer became a man about town in Detroit, despite being just 19 years old. He would sneak in, or be allowed in because he was 6-foot-8, to Baker's Keyboard Lounge to check out jazz legends such as Wes Montgomery and George Benson, Pharoah Sanders, and Miles Davis.

"[Security] would always give me hell at the door, 'You know you're not old enough to be in here.' They all knew who I was because they would come to the games too. Man, the University of Detroit was happening, because we played everybody.

"This watered-down schedule we have now…. We played Notre Dame twice. We played Marquette twice. We played Villanova. We played them all. We were independent.

"And I'm part of the Detroit scene because they have to see me entertain before they entertain. Willie Horton [of the Tigers], all of those guys came to our games."

It was Utopia for Spencer. He was a national celebrity, Olympic gold medalist, 6-foot-8 with a perfect afro, and playing in a city that appreciated its Black achievers. It was light years away from Mississippi.

"Black folks was living large, man. They was making $20 per hour in the auto industry, and if you work in the auto industry you can get a new ride every two years," he said.

It was Motor town, Buick Electra 225s cruising the streets was common. For the local pimps, players, and hustlers, Cadillac was the automobile of choice.

And in an era where numbers running and gambling was prevalent and quite illegal, it would have been conceivable for Spencer to be approached by some local "businessmen" about perhaps point shaving or affecting the Detroit score.

They never approached Spencer. What's more, he said the streets protected him.

"You see Detroit is a city, you were very well protected as an athlete or entertainer," he said. "Because the entertainer couldn't hardly get their drugs because there's a code. So they would never ask me to do that because you could mess up your career. 'I don't want to be a pimp on the corner saying I messed up Spencer Haywood's career.' So they protected me.

"That was the Black code of honor that we used to have, that we would never allow one of our own to go down like that. Because they had had experiences with it with Reggie Harding."

Harding was the first ever NBA player drafted without playing in college. A Detroit native, Harding was selected in the fourth round by the Pistons in 1962 and then the sixth round, again by the Pistons, in 1963. A 7-footer with immense potential, Harding couldn't resist the street life, and became known more for his fascination with guns and running with local hustlers during his time with the Pistons.

He was shot dead at a Detroit intersection in 1972 at age 30. His was the preventative story about the young, talented, and impressionable athlete unable to resist the streets. Spencer wasn't going to be Reggie Harding.

"I know I was well protected," he said. "Man, I couldn't even get ladies."

Spencer planned to remain at Detroit for his final three years. But he'd committed to the school on the condition that his mentor, Robinson, would become head coach, and when that didn't happen, things changed.

"I thought I was gonna play two more [seasons] but they reneged on the deal during the season," he said. "And all of the boosters flipped on me. They was nice to me and all of sudden they were talking about, 'You can't transfer because you can't afford to lose another year.' They started treating me like I was a criminal [and] Will was so hurt and you know it affected me."

The promised hiring would have made Robinson the first Division I Black head coach, but after the Titans finished 16–10, Bob Calihan was forced into retirement after 21 years as coach and Detroit athletic director Fred Shadrick began a national search that did not include Robinson.

Spencer felt he was lured to Detroit on an empty promise to give Robinson the coaching job but university president Father Malcolm J. Carron never intended to hire Robinson, who had become a high school coaching legend and would have established a strong local recruiting base for the school.

Athletic director Shadrick passed on Robinson, saying, according to *Sports Illustrated*, "Sure, Will is a fine man. But we wanted someone with a big-time college background, someone with national contacts."

So instead he opted for Don Haskins, who led Texas Western, with an all-Black starting lineup, to the NCAA Championship over all-White Kentucky, a run that inspired the movie *Glory Road*. But Haskins was peppered with questions about how he would deal with a mostly Black team in the North.

"Now everybody was surprised when Texas Western won that thing," Spencer said. "It was like, 'Aw shit, these Blacks gonna take over here now, goddammit.' Historians talk about how they won it and it opened up the flood gates for Black players. Yeah right."

Feeling uncomfortable about the line of questioning and making such a dramatic change, Haskins resigned the position after 48 hours and returned to Texas Western.

Shadrick then decided on a coach named Jim Harding, a fiery man known for his excruciating practices and bench tirades. What's more, Harding had just been fired by the Minnesota Pipers of the American Basketball Association after a series of anger incidents.

Harding had previous college coaching stints at Loyola (Louisiana) and La Salle. He had also led Loyola to the NCAA Tournament. But that was hardly enough to convince Spencer to stay for another season. He felt personally betrayed and deceived by the Detroit administration, lured to the school with hopes of playing for his adoptive father.

Robinson, now 58, felt his time to get a Division I job was running out and he had his heart set on the Detroit job, coaching in his backyard with the ability to recruit his players.

"They brought in this guy named Jim Harding and our first meeting, he [verbally] attacked me," Spencer said. "I was like, *What the hell? I don't even know this guy.* And [he's taking about] how things are going to change and what he's going to do. I'm like a first-team All-American.

"Now dude, I got some shit here. I ain't no slave. C'mon. So I told Will and I told my boys, 'I don't want to play for this guy. Cause we gonna have a problem, we gonna have a major problem.' [And he's thinking], 'Every time he looks at me, he's gonna think, "I took his dad's job," so there's going to be some friction.' Like they thought because they had a lot of Blacks on the team we needed a slave driver, you know?"

ABA standout Connie Hawkins, who played for Harding that ill-fated season for the Minnesota Pipers, told Spencer's buddy Sonny Dove of the Pistons that Harding had issues with several of his players with the Pipers. He was fired twice in that 1968–69 season, believe it or not, getting canned for an incident after 26 games and then again later in the year. (A year after Spencer departed, Harding was accused by his players of psychological abuse and they threatened to boycott games.)

Spencer said Calihan, whom the school eventually named its arena after, stepped down because he believed Robinson would be named coach. Shadrick reneged on the agreement.

Robinson stayed at Pershing for another season before being named coach at Illinois State, becoming the first African American Division I head coach.

With an athletics director he didn't trust, a coach who had a history of anger issues, and no Robinson to guide him, there was little reason for Spencer to stay in college. The University of Detroit got old quickly for Spencer, who felt like he was a pawn, used to upgrade the basketball program with little choice of staying because hardship cases weren't allowed.

"All of a sudden they flipped on us, man," Spencer said. "Before it was like, 'Black folks are alright, we're going to be okay with this.' But this was the first Black coach in NCAA history we were [talking about] here; this wasn't just some normal little shit here. But they flipped on us and they went back to [Mississippi]."

Each time Spencer felt overt racism, he was rudely reminded of his Mississippi roots. And he was crushed to find out that racism existed this far north too, even in apparently progressive Detroit. Robinson was a great coach when he was tutoring high school prospects for college, but now they were saying he lacked the experience and fortitude to lead a major university program on his own. That's how Spencer viewed it.

Shadrick hired someone who looked like him and reminded him of him. Robinson was a little too tanned for the job. Coaching Pershing High School wasn't threatening to Robinson's White counterparts, but the University of Detroit was truly afraid to take a chance on

Robinson, and they bet because of the rules that prohibited players from leaving school and going directly to the NBA, that Spencer would be relegated to playing his final two years.

"I loved school; when I started [at Detroit] I never thought I would leave early," he said. "Never. I don't care if I was the greatest athlete in the world. Because Will Robinson, he's a coach, I could never think like that. When we got messed over at the University of Detroit, that's when we switched the concept. Ain't no fairness in this.

"We had such a powerful thing in Detroit. Think about this, we had George Gervin. We had a bunch of dudes that would have made the University of Detroit the mecca of basketball. And they snatched it right out from us because of race."

7

A CHANGE IS GONNA COME

WHAT SHADRICK DIDN'T EXPECT OR ANTICIPATE was that there would be another contender for Spencer besides the NBA, which had no intention in 1969 of allowing a hardship case into its league. In 1969, the NBA was a 14-team league that was slow to embrace change, especially a brash Black superstar who sought to enter the league at age 20.

The American Basketball Association, which began in 1967, didn't hold such conservative views. The ABA sought to challenge the NBA, even if that meant challenging conventional thinking about the style of play, hardship cases, the three-point shot, and even the color of the ball.

The ABA is exactly what players in Spencer's situation needed to foster their quest to play professional basketball before their college eligibility ended. However, it wasn't legal for a player who had not completed his eligibility or waited four full years after high school to play professional basketball.

Of course, those were NBA rules. ABA owners, most of them seeking financial stability for their fledging teams, sought to challenge the NBA by offering lucrative contracts to players. What's more, the ABA drafted Providence guard Jimmy Walker, Houston center Elvin Hayes, and UCLA center Lew Alcindor first overall in the first three years of its draft, in an attempt to lure one of those players to ditch the NBA.

The closest the ABA came to attracting one of those players was Alcindor, a New York native who the Nets felt they held an advantage in recruiting by giving the UCLA center an opportunity to play close to home. Unfortunately for the Nets, their bid for Alcindor was lower than the $1.4 million offered by the NBA's Milwaukee Bucks, who won a coin toss with the Phoenix Suns and won the first pick.

Alcindor accepted Milwaukee's offer and the Nets were left empty. But the ABA had no issue with trying to outdo its more conservative counterpart.

Spencer said the ABA considered going after LSU point guard Pete Maravich, another underclassman, but it required convincing Pete's father, Press, to allow him to make that jump. (Maravich was drafted third overall by the NBA's Atlanta Hawks in 1970).

Looking to make a splash and without the restrictive rules of the NBA, ABA owner Bill Ringsby, a trucking mogul who named his Denver team the Rockets after his line of trucks, contacted Spencer about the possibility of making the unprecedented jump to the league for the 1969–1970 season.

"Ricky Mount can't play and Calvin Murphy can play, but he ain't got that kind of impact," Spencer said about the ABA's decision to choose him.

Mount was a stellar college player at Purdue but he chose to stay in school for his senior year and ended up being the No. 1 overall pick of the ABA's Indiana Pacers in 1970. Murphy was one of the most prolific scorers in NCAA history, actually averaging nearly 50 points per game in his junior-varsity stint for Niagara (freshmen were not allowed to play varsity) and 38.2 points in his sophomore season. But Murphy was 5-foot-9 and wasn't going to make the splash the ABA desired.

So it was the idea of Mike Storen, who was co-owner and GM of the Kentucky Colonels (whose daughter Hannah Storm would become a popular sports broadcaster) who devised the idea of luring Spencer into the ABA.

"He was worried about the NCAA, the NBA, and everybody else coming after [him] for finding an underclassman to play ball before their four years were up," Spencer said. "So [he'd have] to have a real good hit for the press conference."

So it was Storen's idea not only to sign Spencer, taking him out of destitute conditions (the term "hardship"), but they were going to make John McLendon the ABA's first Black head coach.

McLendon had become a legend coaching in Black colleges and had actually coached the Cleveland Pipers of the defunct American Basketball League in the early 1960s (a team owned by George Steinbrenner, future owner of the New York Yankees).

Storen felt that hiring McLendon would relieve some of the pressure and scrutiny the signing of Spencer may bring. It was perhaps a half-hearted version of civil rights for the ABA, but the prize in the deal was Spencer. McLendon had bonded with Spencer as an assistant coach under Hank Iba.

The fit seemed natural—even though it wasn't for the right intentions—for McLendon to coach the Rockets.

"This was like a big plot, man," Spencer said. "They brought him in and they bought me in and everybody [the NBA, NCAA] got nervous because they didn't want to make it like, 'We stopping somebody from playing.'

"I was the perfect [hardship] candidate because my mother was picking cotton for $2 a day in Mississippi—my whole family [was]. And I couldn't survive under the college rules. I could have survived, but [the ABA] made it seem like, 'If they don't get no reparations, no money, they ain't gonna make it.'"

Helping Spencer's case in this controversial move was the fact that he was less than a year removed from leading Team USA to an Olympic gold medal. So does the good ol' US of A really want an Olympic hero enduring another year of college, when it was possible for him to make enough money to ensure his mother wouldn't have to pick another bale of cotton?

It was a convincing argument, even though Spencer knew it was utter bullshit. His family would have survived if he had returned to Detroit. They weren't suffering, but the lure of playing professionally, especially when the University of Detroit had betrayed his beloved Will Robinson, made it an easy decision.

Why the Denver Rockets? The best way to legitimize the decision was to call Spencer a regional selection, since he had played at nearby Trinidad Junior College. So the ABA had its argument and reasoning lined up. Spencer was the perfect target. He was young, wildly athletic, talented, and unable to play in the NBA.

"Denver had stability and everything else, because the eyes are gonna be on the ABA now," he said. "We need to have a strong team with a good background. Because I won my gold medal from Trinidad, so I'm a Colorado guy. So there I was, off to Denver.

"There was a lot of diabolical plotting going on. It wasn't just like, 'Hey, we're gonna find this guy?' All of the owners were in collusion with Denver. Because the ABA was gonna shut their doors, remember. Because if they hadn't gotten me, they had no way to compete with the NBA and get any draft picks, because all of the draft picks would go to the NBA. The money wasn't right. They needed a gimmick. And they looked at this like, 'We can get them for two years or three years and then they can go to the NBA.'

"Once they signed me, they were able to get George Gervin, Julius Erving, George McGinnis, Moses Malone. They got a lineup of all of these underclassmen."

Spencer had no hesitation about making the jump. He had played against enough NBA players in those Detroit pickup games to know he could dominate professional competition.

There was nothing on a basketball court to stop Spencer from playing the game he loved. Nothing on a basketball court could stop him from seeking to pull his family out of Mississippi poverty and chasing his dream of playing in the NBA.

The only thing stopping Spencer from playing in the NBA was the NBA itself. It was the beginning of a difficult, tumultuous relationship that would exist for nearly 50 years. Spencer knew the next step to the NBA would be to play in the fledging ABA, and he knew his talent had turned him in to an expensive pawn in the emerging battle between two professional basketball leagues.

It wasn't slavery, or even close, but the fact that Spencer was being treated like expensive property by a group of rich White owners wasn't lost on him. He had become hardened to the system, dismissive of any promises from those who said they had his best interests at heart. If Spencer was going to enter this system, it was going to be on his terms.

So on August 23, 1969, Spencer signed a three-year, $450,000 contract with the Denver Rockets to begin his professional basketball career.

"I was like, 'I'm ready—and I get some money too?'" he said. "'Shit, I'ma kill these dudes.' Then I picked up my cotton-picking attitude in that Mile High altitude. The only thing that John McLendon said is: 'Ain't nobody ever gonna catch your Black ass.'"

Spencer was constantly reminded of his Mississippi upbringing in each stage of his life. Such as in Denver, when running Green Lake Trail was reminiscent of running the train tracks of Silver City to Belzoni, Mississippi, and Spencer said he would run that trail all day. He was free, young, and ambitious.

Spencer scored 30 points in his first professional game with the Rockets, a 109–103 loss to the New Orleans Buccaneers at the Denver Auditorium. Basketball had always come easy and the 20-year-old Spencer dominated the ABA, turning in one of the more remarkable rookie seasons in professional sports history.

But Ringsby expected victories, and McLendon began this job on a short leash. Now that the Rockets had secured Spencer, McLendon had no leverage to keep his job if he didn't win immediately. He was fired after only 28 games (9–19 record), and for the second time in two years, Spencer felt betrayed, as another White authority figure had broken the heart of a mentor just to broker his services. It felt like exploitation.

"They got the player, that's all it was," he said. "Once they got me, got the team rolling, got everything moving, [then] they fired John McLendon and give the job to Joe Belmont, who was a referee before. And the team rolled like champs, because [McLendon] had built us up to that point. And then the racism comes in, saying, 'Well we're going for the championship in the ABA and we've got a Black coach? C'mon now, shit. This is 1969.'"

Of Belmont, who was 35 when he took the job, Spencer said: "He didn't know shit. You know the system works. The brother goes out there and do all the work and then they move him out and somebody comes in and they take the system and run off. He was a referee. Every play, every thing we ran was John McLendon. The style of play—press you from end to end and run you until you couldn't walk—that's where Dean Smith got all of his coaching from and McLendon got his from James Naismith in Kansas. Ain't this shit deep?" McLendon attended the University of Kansas in the mid-1930s, where Naismith was the athletics director. But because of segregation, McLendon was not allowed to play on the basketball team.)

As for the ABA experience, Spencer said he loved playing in Denver. It was a progressive city with more than a million people, light years from Mississippi and less congested than Detroit. Spencer could just play basketball.

"I was putting up some numbers and we was winning," he said. "Every home game was a sellout. We was the only team in the ABA that had sellouts—the only one."

Spencer played an astonishing 45.3 minutes per game for the Rockets, meaning he was on the court approximately 90 percent of the time. So much for load management. He led the league in 11 statistical categories, including scoring (30.0 points), rebounding (19.5), and field goals (986), winning the league's Most Valuable Player Award. He was the original rookie sensation, dazzling fans in the ABA's smaller arenas, convention halls, and civic centers around the 11-team league.

"I didn't come off the court and I didn't want to come off the court," he said. "So for young guys, I'm playing 45-plus minutes a game and I'm getting 30 points and 20 rebounds. This is work. I was like Br'er Rabbit."

"Br'er Rabbit" was another Mississippi reference, but it predates Spencer's days in Silver City. The "Br'er Rabbit" was an African folk story about a character who was able to survive despite dire circumstances and at the same time occasionally pester and defeat his enemy, which symbolically was White slaveowners.

Late–19th century fiction writer Joel Chandler Harris used the "Br'er Rabbit" in his Uncle Remus book series. "Br'er Rabbit" was the main character in those stories, narrated by the fictional Uncle Remus, who would tell slavery tales of the 1850s. The "Br'er Rabbit" character was an agitator, and in some cases a troublemaker who would sometimes pay dearly for his rambunctious style.

It was apparent Spencer identified with this character, and to many Southern Blacks, the "Br'er Rabbit" was viewed as a hero because he didn't fall in line with the system. That was symbolic of Spencer, who knew his biggest battles in the near future wouldn't occur close to any basketball court.

"[After the] season in Denver, we had this big press conference with the commissioner [Jack Dolph] saying, 'We have the highest-paid player in professional basketball, right here in Denver, the ABA is paying big money," Spencer said. "'We gave Spencer Haywood a contract for $1.9 million over five years.'"

While the money sounded impressive, Spencer claims he saw very few of those dollars. The ABA was still an unstable league, with teams folding and relocating every one of its 10 years.

"The shit was so fraudulent, because they were paying me $75,000 a year and the rest of the money was put into Wall Street [mutual fund] at $10,000 per year for five years," Spencer said.

What Spencer discovered was that most of his $1.9 million would be deferred in payments of $75,000 for 20 years, meaning Spencer would receive the final payment of his contract at age 40 in 1989. And of course, $75,000 in 1989 would be worth much less than $75,000 in 1969.

Spencer hired attorney Al Ross to review the contract, and said he knew he was being hustled. The only way for these ABA team to afford to offer such lucrative contracts is if the payments were deferred for many years after the contract expired. What happens if the Rockets folded? Who would pay Spencer the rest of his owed money?

At 20 years old, Spencer was the victim of a Detroit-style hustle.

"There's a slight catch in it, if Wall Street goes bad, I don't get shit," he said. "And the other catch they had written into the contract—because I didn't have no attorney [when I signed], I just figured they just loved me because I'm the MVP—is that for me to receive the $1.9 million, I would have to be employed by Ringsby's truck line, who owns the Rockets."

And the contract stipulated Spencer wouldn't begin receiving his money from those mutual-fund investments until he was 50.

"So basically, it was bullshit," he said. "I would have had to work for Ringsby until I died. I didn't have any managerial experience, so I figured, *Shit, they would put me on the truck*."

Ringsby died in 1981 and his trucking company eventually folded in 1984, meaning Spencer would have never received even close to the $1.9 million he agreed upon when he signed that initial contract.

"Race always played a part," he said. "They just won't do right. I hate to say it. Why would you do some shit like that? Why would you give a fraudulent contract? Why would you do such an evil thing if you got the MVP? And the boy who's making you all this money? Why would you do that shit?

"And when I did get an attorney, the first thing out of [Ringsby's] mouth was, 'You get your Jew ass out of here and take this nigger with you.' And they wouldn't even speak to us because they said, 'We've got a contract. We ain't doing nothing.'"

Soon enough, Denver wasn't such a peaceful place for Spencer. He was experiencing the same racial issues he'd experienced in Detroit and especially Mississippi.

"They hate my ass, they only wanted my service," he said.

After such a glorious first season with the Rockets, Spencer felt discriminated and disrespected as a man. Ross then had the idea of reaching out to the NBA, which had a handful of expansion teams looking to make a splash, to see if Spencer wanted to make history.

Seattle SuperSonics owner Sam Schulman promised Spencer he would honor his remaining Rockets contract with real dollars, not deferment payments. And Spencer would get to fulfill his lifelong dream of playing in the NBA.

But the NBA did not allow players who weren't four years removed from high school. Spencer, however, had no choice but to challenge that rule and take on the National Basketball Association, because the ABA had betrayed him, just like the University of Detroit.

"I said, 'I'll go over [to the NBA],' but [according to their rules, I was] going to have to sit out a year, which I was in no mood for, to be sitting out," he said. "If I sat out for another year, [then] the NBA put me into the draft—which they did after I won the case.

"I wanted to play in Seattle, but I was going to have to win this case. I was going to have to fight my way into the NBA. For this Mississippi boy, nothing came easy. I knew I couldn't just sign with the Sonics. The big boys in the NBA were going to have something to say about that."

8

HAYWOOD V. NATIONAL BASKETBALL ASSOCIATION

NOW UNDER THE **NBA** BYLAWS, Spencer would need to sit out a full season before playing, because he would then be four years removed from high school. But that wasn't exactly Spencer's plan. He had no intention on missing the season, but he needed a maverick NBA owner to support his cause, even though it would be an unpopular decision amongst his ownership brethren.

The NBA was deathly afraid of opening its doors to underclassman. The league was filled with conservative owners who didn't want to open the flood gates to 19-year-olds who may be unprepared for the life. Spencer proved he was physically ready for the NBA, but he had little support for an NBA jump, other than Schulman. That, however, was all he needed for now.

Eventually, expansion owners Jerry Colangelo (Phoenix), Dick Klein (Chicago), and Wesley Pavalon and Marvin Fishman (Milwaukee) were the only owners who supported Spencer's entry into the league. And that's because they knew the key to uplifting their infant franchises to compete with the league's powers was to sign underclassman.

Spencer understood the deal, though. He knew the old White NBA ownership hierarchy didn't want hardship cases because most of those players who would choose to leave college early would be Black. The NBA was still a majority White league in the early 1970s, and Spencer threatened to shift the culture and the racial demographic of the league.

"You had a bunch of old people in the NBA like that bastard that owned the Lakers, Jack Kent Cooke," Spencer said. Then, imitating Cooke, "'We don't want no young players in here. Our league is going to be permeated with Black players. Our fan base will not support us.'

"I was like, *Ain't that some shit.*"

So the league filed an affidavit to prevent Spencer from signing with the Sonics, threatening to ban Spencer and levy fines against Schulman if Spencer appeared in a Seattle uniform.

Spencer and Al Ross were preparing for such an action and they filed an injunction in the United States District Court for the Central District of California, claiming NBA owners collaborated to stop him from entering the league and were violating the Sherman Antitrust Act. That Act prevents companies from conspiring for anticompetitive agreements.

Spencer's lawsuit claimed NBA owners purposely denied him an opportunity to play because they were essentially racist. And he had a point. Signing the best player in the ABA would obviously make any NBA team better, so why wouldn't they touch Spencer?

The District Court ruled in Spencer's favor, saying: "If Spencer is unable to continue to play professional basketball for Seattle, he will suffer irreparable injury in that a substantial part of his playing career will have been dissipated; his physical condition, skills, and coordination will deteriorate from lack of high-level competition; his public acceptance as a superstar will diminish to the detriment of his career; his self-esteem and his pride will have been injured and a great injustice will be perpetrated on him."

It was apparent that many of the league's powerful owners were fearful of the NBA adding more Black players on hardship cases. It obviously had nothing to do with Spencer's talent. He was one the best players in the world, but it was going to require the highest court to secure Spencer's NBA dream. Again, it would require patience and fortitude.

"We don't want to end up with the Niggerbockers," Spencer said, referring to what some journalists and fans called the Knicks team he was on, which had only two White players, Glen Gondrezick and John Rudd, both benchwarmers. (The next year, Gondrezick and Rudd would both be gone and the 1979–1980 Knicks would be referred to as the "all-Black Knicks.") "You know that's what they called us, right?"

Schulman disregarded the legal red tape and signed Spencer on December 30, 1970, 40 games into the season. Spencer, still 21, said he was uncomfortable being tabbed as Seattle's savior. The Sonics were an NBA neophyte, having finished near the bottom of the Western Division in their first three seasons.

Schulman thought he had his franchise player, and brought Spencer to a city that was still very much new to professional sports. The Pilots lasted only one season (1969) before moving to Milwaukee.

The Seattle Seahawks and Mariners didn't come to fruition until 1976 and 1977, respectively.

While the Sonics featured perennial All-Star Lenny Wilkens, who was in his early thirties as their star player and coach, Spencer would become Seattle's first legitimate superstar.

"I'm coming into Seattle and I'm saving this shit—I got this," he said. "Because first of all, when they had the press conference there. All these people show up... and I'm still kinda country... and they were talking to me about all the beautiful girls here and I said, 'Well I don't see no Black women here.' They took it as an insult. My dumb ass, I was so stupid.

"They were so embracive and they were so protective."

Spencer, after the injunction cleared him to play, make his Seattle debut on January 4, 1971, in a game at Milwaukee against the Bucks, who had Oscar Robertson and Kareem Abdul-Jabbar. Spencer scored 14 points in the loss.

In a January 9 road game at Cincinnati, Spencer played two minutes and then was kicked out of the arena by Royals officials.

The next month was spent with the two sides trading injunctions, culminating in the NBA appealing to the Supreme Court, which forced Spencer to sit for nearly two weeks.

He stayed at his plush hotel room at the Washington Towers in late February 1971, waiting for the final decision.

"It was really hard because I didn't know it was going to be that kind of battle," he said. "So I'm sitting up in the hotel and I'm like, *Wow, I just want to play.*"

Spencer snuck out of the seclusion of his room to check out trumpeter Hugh Masekela performing downtown, but then it was back to his personal exile. He had the money. He had the lifestyle. But it meant nothing without basketball.

"I was looking out my window wondering, *When am I ever gonna play again?*" he said. "I was getting paid. Everything was fine, but then it became about playing and it brought me down. And all of this stuff is done publicly. You got [people] in Seattle that talk about the injunction. They would come on the mic when I was on the road, 'Ladies and Gentlemen, we got this injunction and this man can't play and he's got to leave this court!'"

Spencer was forced to leave a few games before the opening tip when those injunctions arrived. He was embarrassed and humiliated.

"I enjoyed playing because it was something I liked," he said. "The NBA players, they were so confused, because the owners said to the players—great players like Chet Walker—'You gotta break his jaw when he comes around because this guy is putting y'all out of business. You think of all the new players that's going to be coming in, they're going to be 19 and 20, y'all gotta go.' The old heads in the league, that's what they thought of me."

What confused Spencer was that he felt the owners were turning his own brethren, Black players, against him. Many veteran NBA players believed Spencer was a threat to their jobs, and he had to withstand a series of cheap shots that he feels were instructed by the league's White power structure.

"They were clotheslining me and shit," Spencer said. "And if it wasn't for Tom Meschery, the Masher, [it would've been even worse], because he would knock them out."

Meschery was a Russian immigrant who was 11 years Spencer's senior. And he was one of the NBA's main enforcers in the 1960s, finishing in the top 10 in personal fouls six times in the decade.

"He just took it upon himself; 'Nobody is going to mess with you,'" Spencer said. "'I'll fight 'em until I die right here.' Rod Thorn would pick me up and we would just talk, and since we were both country boys, we had that thing going on."

Wilkens, who was with Spencer for his first two years in Seattle, served as his mentor.

"Lenny was just my champion of champions," Spencer said. "He was teaching me so much, [and] how to deal with the situation. And Sam Schulman, the owner of the Sonics, he took it personally like I was his son, like, 'This is my boy. I'm not going to let nobody mess with [him]. I'll lose my franchise on this.' It was that kind of atmosphere."

Spencer also struck up a close friendship with a kid named Rick Welts, who began as the Sonics ballboy and then worked for the public relations staff. Welts would eventually become president and CEO of the Golden State Warriors.

"Me and him bonded because I was closer to his age than I was with the other guys," he said. "Those guys were drinking beer. I don't want no beer. I'm an athlete. So when the hour and half, two hours were up [in practice], they were like, 'I gotta go home. I got a family.' So Rick Welts and I would just ball. I would stay in the gym because I wasn't used to working for just two hours and just [going] home.

"I'd stay in the gym and work on my game and he was like the perfect guy for it because he would push me to work. So there we were, two young boys in the gym."

Spencer also took classes at the University of Washington and Seattle University and was able to blend in with the students. That was his element.

Spencer could do nothing because he was advised to refrain from any retaliation. His legal team of Frank Rothman, former California governor Pat Brown, and Jack Quinn told him that any violence would jeopardize his case.

"They said, 'Whatever you do, you're going to have the [college] people coming after you,]' because I had Duke and all these major university people, [they] tried to punk me when I was going to the hotel. They would get all up in my face hoping that I would do something, so then I'd be out," he said.

"And then I would get on the floor and the players' union did not support me. [Union general counsel] Larry Fleisher and the union were like, 'Shit, you're going to put everybody else out of a job.' [The attitude was] 'You have all these young players coming and this is the guy you've got to stop right now. Otherwise you're going to be out of the job.'"

It was the first time that Spencer felt like a martyr amongst his fellow NBA players, including the Black players. They didn't admire his journey or his decision to leave school early and sign with an NBA team without the league's approval.

Spencer felt that decision strained his relationship with the league and many players for more than 30 years. He never forgot how he was treated.

"The Black players were like, 'Oh no, man, you gotta go back to school for a couple more years; you don't belong in here,'" he said.

"And I got 40 points on them and they're still telling me I don't belong. I get 40 and 15 [rebounds] and they're telling me I don't belong?"

Spencer knew it had nothing to do with basketball. He was the biggest threat the league had seen since integration. He represented a new breed of player, the street-ball stars whose games were skilled enough to compete and dominate as teenagers. Spencer was a basketball wunderkind, but because of his decision to leave school and challenge the establishment and its slave-mentality system, he was viewed as an unwanted rebel.

Still, Spencer enjoyed himself in his new home. Seattle was a blend of liberalism, diversity, and natural beauty that he had never experienced. Seattle fancied itself America's best-kept secret, a city on the rise. And Spencer was one of the city's most identifiable personalities.

"It was like a novelty, NBA ball at that time for them in Seattle," he said. "They were just drinking their coffee and going over the floating bridge. But they came out in droves. It was party city. Our games were something special. It was exciting. It was beautiful.

"And they showed the motherly love. It was deeper than just the player love. That's why I when I went to New York [in 1975] I was so hurt. Because they had loved me so strongly and I bonded with them. It was a painful journey."

Seattle is where Spencer spent his best basketball seasons.

"There was no racism, there was no nothing there," he said. "I never experienced that there. Everybody was treated equal. It was something else."

Spencer viewed Seattle as paradise. He built a lake home in the Lake Washington area and brought three of his brothers and two sisters to live with him, making the place comfortable and fulfilling a promise that the sibling who made it biggest would take care of their brothers and sisters.

What would have made Seattle even more like home is if he could have convinced his mother, Eunice, to relocate from Silver City to live with him. Spencer flew her out and showed her the luxurious house, but it wasn't Mississippi. Culturally, Eunice was completely uncomfortable, despite the beauty.

"'Boy, you're living in the water,'" she would tell him. "What kind of fool would build his house in the water when you got all this land? The killer of the deal was the floating bridge. She was like, 'No, I ain't never heard of no such thing as a floating bridge. What kind of life y'all living up here?'"

Eunice's first plane trip was to see her son in Seattle and she ate up the first-class treatment. Her superstar son wanted so badly for Mama to enjoy her visit and perhaps consider moving there. But once Eunice saw the size of the churches and the expanding metropolitan city, she was ready to get back to Silver City.

"I wanted her to live her life in glory," he said. "But she was like, 'How can I live better than what I'm living? I got a new Cadillac, I got a house that matches everybody's house, and I got money in the bank too. I done died and gone to heaven and you're going to try to move me some place [else].'

"She wasn't going for that shit."

Spencer worked for this dream. He wanted his mother close to him, but those Mississippi roots are hard to shake. His mother worried about the people she drove to her local church. She was attached to Mississippi. As much as Spencer resented his upbringing, hated those

White men who oppressed him, for Eunice, it was the only existence she had ever known.

Seattle, despite all of its beauty, diversity, and model weather, was a foreign place to a Southern woman, and she would remain only a visitor.

"I worked all those years to have all this stuff and she was going to be here with all of her kids in Seattle, but I understood where she was coming from," Spencer said. "Because she had never even been to Jackson [Mississippi's largest city]. That's 'the big city.' My mother hadn't been to Jackson, hardly, you know? That's a cultural change. She wasn't ready for it and she didn't want it.

"And to be quiet as it's kept, she used to say, 'Y'all are living in Babylon, baby. Just like in the Bible.'"

His rookie season would be the final time Eunice would visit Seattle. She insisted Spencer come visit Mississippi. Every summer during his career, Spencer would go home to Silver City and spend those blazing Mississippi days with Eunice.

Using the Cadillac he bought her, Spencer would scoop up all of Eunice's friends with her in the passenger's side and drive to Sunday church.

"You go over there and pick up Mrs. Jackson," she would tell him.

"I didn't come here to hang with her, I came here to hang with you," he would tell her.

"You know, you're getting too big for your britches," she responded.

Spencer never attended court during the entire legal proceedings. He had his legal representation at the sessions while he waited by the phone at times to find out if he was even eligible to play that night for the Sonics. When the case reached the Supreme Court, one of those judges who heard the case was the legendary Thurgood Marshall.

Like his times in Detroit, when he rubbed elbows with the likes of Smokey Robinson, Melvin Franklin, and Marvin Gaye, the young Spencer found himself in the company of one the most influential men of the 20ᵗʰ century.

Spencer's old coach, Will Robinson, was one of Jackie Robinson's escorts when Robinson broke into the major leagues and traveled city to city with the Brooklyn Dodgers and needed to stay in all-Black neighborhoods.

Will Robinson was Jackie Robinson's liaison in Detroit, and Jackie introduced Will to Marshall, who was part of a group of judges, such Damon Keith and Edward Bell, who would meet occasionally in the city of Detroit. More than 20 years later, Will Robinson promised Spencer a chance to meet Marshall when the Sonics played the Baltimore Bullets.

"I didn't understand the impact," Spencer said. "Shit, I had another game. I was so stupid. I think about all this now and boy I was sort of dense. I was a young boy. I didn't know. I couldn't understand the impact.

"I was just walking the walk, man. I was at the right place at the right time. My mom would always say, 'You were built for this; you were born for this. I knew that from Day One.'"

Will Robinson also served as Spencer's primary motivator, insisting that Spencer belonged amongst kings and dignitaries like Marshall.

But that night in Baltimore, Spencer said he was thinking about how good that filet mignon was.

"I know this shit sounds crazy but I'm just telling you straight up," he said. "I was 21, man. And I had went through so much shit by the time I went up to Detroit. I win the state championship, become the crown prince of Detroit, go to the Olympics, come back, save the city, then go to the ABA, save that, and then go to the NBA and start a whole new revolution, and I'm sitting there with Thurgood and Will, saying, 'Man, I wonder what kind of steak they got here.'

"There was so much happening around me that I didn't have time to think about that stuff."

By this time, the case had become anticlimactic for Spencer. He didn't believe in the system. He didn't understand why he couldn't just play ball and why these powerful men with multimillion-dollar businesses and investments were so concerned about a cotton-picker from Mississippi.

As the case rose to the Supreme Court, the NBA made one final plea to keep Spencer from playing for the Sonics until his college class had graduated in June of 1971.

Prior to a March 8 game with Milwaukee for a second matchup with Abdul-Jabbar and Robertson, Spencer received a call from Rothman that the Supreme Court had voted 7–2 to uphold the District Court's ruling, allowing Spencer to play for good.

Marshall was one of the judges that voted yes.

Supreme Court Justice William O. Douglas wrote in court's decision:

"To dissolve the stay would preserve the interest and integrity of the playoff system, as I have indicated. Should there not be a decision prior to beginning of the playoffs and should Seattle make the playoffs then the District Court could fashion whatever relief it deems

equitable. In view of the equities between the parties, 28 U. S. C. §
1651 (a), I have decided to allow the preliminary injunction of the
District Court to be reinstated. The status quo provided by the Court
of Appeals is the status quo before applicant signed with Seattle. The
District Court preserved the status quo prior to the NBA's action
against Seattle and Spencer. That is the course I deem most worthy
of this interim protection. The stay will issue.

"Stay Granted."

It was a victory for Spencer, but as he walked through the tunnel
of Milwaukee Arena only to get his customary boos from opposing
fans, he was hugged by Abdul-Jabbar before the team took the floor
to warm up.

It was an achievement for Spencer and the movement, but all
Spencer wanted to think about was ball. He had no idea the gravity
of his moment or what exactly he had just accomplished. He was an
unintentional pioneer whose contributions to the game would not
be realized for another 25 years.

9

SUPERSONICS, BILL RUSSELL, AND THE BIG CHANGE

THAT FIRST GAME AFTER THE Supreme Court's decision was a special one.

"It was a beautiful game that night," Spencer said. "Because it was the first time I had freedom in two years, basically. To be on the court every day and they talking about, 'We've got an illegal player on the floor' and all that negative shit, and all of a sudden it's being shed by the new king of the NBA [Kareem Abdul-Jabbar] and I'm sort of like the prince of the NBA, so and he's embracing his new friend."

Spencer viewed Abdul-Jabbar's hug as acceptance. Abdul-Jabbar was only in his second NBA season, but he was already the face of the league. He had changed his name, embraced Islam, and taken a considerable amount of criticism for his beliefs. There was a bond there that would help Spencer a decade later.

"So it's like, 'Hey, c'mon in, brother. You did the right thing,'" Spencer said. "Finally somebody likes me. Because he wasn't affected by the situation."

A night before the game, Abdul-Jabbar invited Spencer to his Milwaukee-area home for dinner, and the two shared a deep conversation about Islam.

Abdul-Jabbar started a movement of NBA players who began to embrace Islam during the late stages of the Civil Rights Movement. Spencer started to study the basics of Islam, as he sought to be more socially and religiously conscious.

The experience didn't embitter Spencer, but it did serve as an awakening that racism would follow him from Mississippi to Detroit to Seattle, except the racists didn't wear hoods, they donned suits and governed NBA teams.

Spencer, mentored by former UCLA star and current NBA forward Walt Hazzard (Mahdi Abdul-Rahman), was close to making the total transformation to Islam, and then he called Eunice.

"'Oh baby, baby, baby! Oh my God! You're going to give up Jesus?'" she asked him. "'And you're going to change your name? Don't you know you we've struggled for 400 years to get that name on top and now you're going to throw it away. Take me on to heaven right now!'"

"Oh boy, with all this drama, I'll just keep my name and y'all just call me Abdullah."

So close friends and other Muslims would refer to Spencer as Abdullah during his Seattle years.

Spencer was not a member of the Nation of Islam, the Black-based group that was made popular by Malcolm X (who eventually resigned from the organization) and eventually Muhammad Ali. Spencer, Abdul-Jabbar, Olympic teammate Charlie Scott, and Hazzard studied the teaching of the Quran, which is different than the Nation of Islam.

Spencer said he was also intrigued by Judaism, after having conversations with Sonics owner Sam Schulman.

"I liked having the spiritual base, so I did look at that, but I hadn't been to New York and hung out with the Israelites up in Harlem because I thought Sammy Davis Jr. was just talking shit," he said. "I didn't put two and two together. At that time, Jesus Christ was everything. And with Sammy Davis Jr., he was with Dean Martin and Frank Sinatra, so where's the Judaism?

"My sisters and my family, they wouldn't accept me," Spencer said. "Nah, they know me as Weedie. You can talk that 'As-salamu alaykum' all you want, but I know who you is boy."

That hardly moved Spencer to resent his family. He was the breadwinner and realized how much they depended on him. And in turn he embraced and appreciated their support.

"Heck no," he said. "I loved them more. I wasn't gung ho about the religion, I mostly kept it under wraps. I just went through all those court cases. I knew what was out there. So I didn't just go full throttle with my whole public persona. I just didn't do it."

The only solace during these difficult times was provided by coming home to Seattle, which had adopted Spencer as its first real superstar athlete.

"When I could come home from a real battle, where I didn't play for 10 days because there was an injunction, I come home and go over to 13 Coins [Restaurant] and they would just love me up," he said. "And I had this big, ol' ugly car, so I was recognizable wherever I went, and I went down to get some soul food in the hood and they would give me love. I didn't see White and Black up there. That was the beauty of what I was experiencing.

"So that made it a lot easier, because when I went out on the road, White people would say some horrible shit. I'd come back to Seattle and they'd say the opposite, so I couldn't be mad at White folks."

Spencer became attached to Seattle and he never forgot how the city treated him during these times. Unfortunately for him, that bond would eventually weaken because of basketball.

"Nothing but love, that was a lovefest and I thought, *These corny dudes are going to eventually trade me,*" he said. "*They're gonna turn on me. Because they can't be this nice*—from my experience down South and then in Detroit. It's the same to this day. That's why I like going up there and hanging out with my sisters and all of them. Seattle is something else."

What angered Spencer even more about his journey is that he felt little support from the Black community or fellow Black athletes, other than Abdul-Jabbar. There were no signs of support from Black activists or other NBA players who did not have the opportunity or the courage to follow a similar path and fight the NCAA and NBA.

Perhaps it was jealously of his talent, or a threat that he would start a string of teenagers bombarding the draft and taking jobs. He felt completely ignored, except when he was scoring buckets.

"I was just on an island," he said. "Wilt [Chamberlain] made a joke about it."

"'You stupid,'" Spencer said Chamberlain told him during a conversation in the famous Inglewood Forum Club. "'You think I didn't want to come into the NBA when I left Kansas? I didn't want to fight no case like you and all of that shit.'"

Chamberlain left Kansas after his junior season and instead of fighting to play in the NBA a year before his eligibility was up, he accepted a $50,000 contract from the Harlem Globetrotters. He then entered the 1959 draft, where he was taken by the Philadelphia Warriors.

"You're Wilt Chamberlain!" Spencer said in disbelief about Chamberlain being fearful of the battle.

"'Doesn't matter, son. You know who runs this shit.'"

What disappointed Spencer was that there appeared to be no victories with his victory. He wasn't celebrated. He wasn't viewed as a trailblazer, more like a disruptor. That type of treatment estranged Spencer from most of his brethren.

"I was angry for years," he said. "I just got it off of me maybe, I've been so angry for so many years, so disappointed, the people that I fought for, that I was paving all of this way for, they never liked me. They never knew why they didn't like me. Like somebody done told them, their agent or somebody, 'You stay away from him. Don't talk to that guy, he's trouble.'

"So I had that cloud over me. I couldn't get to nobody, I couldn't talk to nobody. I think when I went to the Hall of Fame, that lifted a lot of burden off of me. [I could] breathe again. You think about all those years, I couldn't breathe."

And then there was the racism. During the early 1970s, Haywood said he heard plenty of discriminating chants from fans and even arena officials during and after the trial. But he was thick-skinned because of his Mississippi upbringing. The remarks pierced him, but he knew responding would ruin any chance of winning the case and retaining his reputation.

"My antenna, my hearing was like—I heard everything and I took it," he said. "Down into my scrotum, past my heart, it was like cutting through to me. People saying some cruel, horrible shit. I couldn't do anything. I had to compartmentalize it. I knew I shouldn't have taken this task on if you can't take the pressure.

"Of course the lawyers and everybody was telling me, 'Jackie [Robinson] went through a lot of shit.' And that was always what they told me, 'Jackie did this, Jackie did that.' Shit, I ain't Jackie Robinson—but I was in a way. But I'm a young dude, I'm 21, what do I know? When they're comparing me to Jackie and I'm like, 'What are you talking about? Jackie Wilson? Get the outta here!'"

In this case, Spencer's childhood prepared him for this new type of hate and disdain. He couldn't respond in Mississippi for fear of being lynched.

"I lived that shit," he said. "I lived slavery. You had to bite your tongue, you had to live with 'Boy, don't you be eyeballing me!' I learned not to look at nobody in their eye."

Spencer said it took Will Robinson a full year to get him to look White people in the eye once he moved to Detroit. In Mississippi, looking at a White person in his eyes, which would be considered menacing or threatening, could mean being murdered.

"I told Will I don't want get punched in the face anymore," he said.

The stress and pain eventually encouraged Spencer to see a psychiatrist and he was diagnosed with Post-Traumatic Stress Disorder.

"I was an outcast," he said. "It was horrible. It was horrible."

While Spencer became an All-Star and superstar during those early years in Seattle, the Sonics didn't win. He was essentially a one-man show. He played in four All-Star Games with the Sonics, was named first-team All-NBA twice, and was top 10 in scoring four times in his five Seattle seasons.

He had achieved great individual success but the question lingered whether a team could be a championship contender with Spencer as its primary option. The Sonics improved during the Wilkens years but the club traded him—despite the fact he was also the coach—to the Cleveland Cavaliers after the 1971–72 season so he could continue his playing career.

"I'm not even in my prime," Spencer said. "I was ready to rock 'n' roll."

Spencer averaged nearly 30 points per game in 1972–73, but the Sonics went through two coaches and won just 26 games. The organization needed a change of direction and Schulman hired all-time great player and trailblazer Bill Russell as coach for the 1973–74 season.

Russell took over the Celtics as player-coach in 1966–67 before leading Boston to consecutive titles in 1968 and 1969. He stepped down to pursue a career in broadcasting, but later said he was ready to coach again. The Sonics finished 36–46 in his first season. Spencer's numbers dropped considerably because he took fewer shots and concentrated more on rebounding.

In 1974–75, Russell led the Sonics to their first playoff appearance as a franchise, as Seattle topped the Detroit Pistons in the first-round mini-series before losing to the eventual champion Golden State Warriors in six games.

But Spencer wasn't himself in that Warriors series. His shoulder was hurt, and he shot only 33.7 percent from the field and missed 11 free throws in the six games. Tom Burleson, a 7-foot-2 rookie from national champion North Carolina State, led the Sonics in scoring during the playoffs.

Fred Brown, a fourth-year guard from Iowa, averaged 21 ppg, just under Spencer's 22.4, so the Sonics believed they had a winning recipe, one which didn't include Spencer dominating the ball. The Sonics were planning to move forward, and that meant either a change of roles for Spencer or a divorce.

After that 1974–75 season, Russell pulled Spencer aside for a heart-to-heart conversation.

"You know Spence, you have a lot of enemies on that team," Russell told him.

Spencer was shocked. He thought he got along with all his teammates.

"I didn't know that," Spencer said. "Guys that I thought was my best, best, best friends were like, 'Get him out of here.' So when Russ [as he called Bill Russell] called me in to talk about it, I took it as an insult and I took it very personal. Like, *I don't want to be here.* Just the idea that you called me in to question me if I liked it in Seattle and shit. I was like, 'I don't know no place else.'

"All of the pain and suffering that I went through has been loved out of me in Seattle. I didn't give Russell an option. I was hurt by the thought of him even bringing me into talk to me about this. 'What is wrong with you? Are you crazy? I don't want to be around any of you son of a bitches.' That's how it ended up."

Spencer suspected jealously had crept into the Sonics' locker room. The organization had drafted Burleson and Brown with top 10 picks, and they felt ready for an expanded role. The Sonics wanted to show they were no longer a one-man show and Spencer felt betrayed by a few particular teammates.

"They were some guys on that team who wanted to be the star and I know who it [was]," he said. "[Fred Brown] had Russ' ear at that time. Not only that, but [my friend from Detroit] John Brisker thought I didn't stand up for him against Russ. [But] Fred [Brown] wanted me out, period. He wanted me out of there.

"That hurt more than a lot of things. Fred was my personal friend. That was one of the main things that happened that really put me through a spin. I was being betrayed by my dear friends.

"So I wind up in New York."

Brown eventually became one of the centerpieces of the 1979 Sonics championship team and an All-Time great Sonic. He made his only All-Star Game in the year after Spencer left. Brisker's playing time decreased during his final two seasons in Seattle and he felt Spencer should have lobbied Russell to get him more playing time.

Brisker was released after the 1974–75 season, his final in the NBA. He was reportedly killed in Uganda in 1979 after he traveled there by invitation of dictator Idi Amin. Brisker is believed to have been killed by a firing squad after Amin's government was overthrown.

Spencer believed his close relationship with Russell, and the fact that he was anointed the team spokesman when it came to issues between his teammates and Russell, led to resentment.

Haywood said he had no issues playing for Russell, who had his issues with coaching after his Celtics days.

Russell resigned from the Sonics in 1977 after owner Sam Schulman demanded that he give up either his head coach or GM duties and take a pay cut, and, after an unsuccessful year, he was fired by the Sacramento Kings in 1988.

"I like Russ," Spencer said. "Because he didn't bitch at me so much. We'd sit at 13 Coins Restaurant and talk basketball, talk about life. He would talk about his experiences with Martin Luther King and I was deep into that stuff. I wanted to know all of the stories. And we also were Mississippi and Louisiana boys, so we had some other shit going on that other players on the team didn't understand."

Like many all-time greats who take up coaching, Russell couldn't figure out why players who had the potential to be great just weren't, and he didn't have the patience to develop them.

"He couldn't understand why Jim McDaniels got this big ol' beautiful shot and don't want to play no defense, don't want to get down in the gritty, the nuthole," Spencer said. "And that ate him alive. And John Brisker, who had all the shit he loved as a player, but they couldn't get along. It was always some little shit that they were going through because they didn't get Russ."

Spencer said Russell would sometimes bring his putter to practice and just putt during the players' wind sprints. He didn't enjoy teaching the game and he became frustrated with players who lacked his drive.

"The players looked at him like the players look at me today," Spencer said. "'What are you talking about? Bill Russell? That was back in the old days when people wore Chuck Taylors.' And he didn't make no big money as a player and Seattle was his new opportunity and it's where he belonged in life at the time. Seattle make you feel really good about yourself out there.

"I gave him respect, but we didn't give him what we should have. We sure didn't. It was always some Goddamn complaining, you know? We were always like, 'He could have did more. He could have did this.' He always compared us to Boston, 'We ain't no Celtics. Those are White boys. We Black guys. Why he give us the same playbook they got?'

"It didn't matter to me. I'm a winner. I ain't used to this. I ain't never played on a team that we didn't get to the playoffs."

In the end, Haywood had many regrets about how he handled his playing career. Instead of a first-ballot Hall of Famer, Haywood played with five different teams and won one NBA title—that dubious season in Los Angeles. It wasn't the journey he envisioned. He didn't fulfill his potential.

The turning point, he said, was leaving Seattle, feeling betrayed and embarrassed by teammates he felt were friends.

"My moodiness and my anger deep down, it scared teams and players and people," he said. "I had it under control up in Seattle, but when I left Seattle, I lost it. I lost my drive and the whole idea that I'm the best [and] I want to stay the best. I don't care what I do, once you put all your love into a place—in Seattle and the Sonics—I wasn't thinking about the business.

"I was thinking about the emotion, my friendship to guys who I lived and died for and the next thing they're gathering up in the big room saying, 'He's got to go!' What the hell? Guys I ride or die with, man. So I should have handled that differently.

"I was betrayed by the city as well. 'You people live up here in this utopia and you don't know about Black folks and when Black folks and dark people get around you, y'all gonna turn, just like you turned on me.' I was taking it out on the wrong people. I was taking it out on Sam Schulman. I was taking it out on Bill Russell. But I never took it out on the players. They weren't about shit."

Haywood even claims years later that in a 25th anniversary recollection of the Sonics history, his 51-point game in 1973 against the Kansas City–Omaha Kings was described as an "unimportant game."

"Now who would do some shit like this?" he said. "Then I found out who the curator of the book was, Fred Brown.

"Fred, man, that is some cruel shit to do."

Leaving Seattle meant also leaving his family. Many of his 10 siblings lived in his Lake Washington home. But heading to New York and living in Manhattan meant they couldn't come with him. They remained in his house, but Spencer lost a sense of security living without his family for the first time.

"I didn't have my sister's cooking; I lost my family after I brought them all together," he said. "I lost them all when I left and went to New York."

Spencer's siblings made a life in Washington. His sister Ivory worked for the city of Seattle for 40 years. His brother Floyd attended college in the area and then played overseas in France. His brothers Andrew and Joe opened an auto shop that flourished for many years.

But Spencer was leaving.

10

THE NIKE STORY

DURING HIS TIME IN SEATTLE, Spencer was approached with a business venture that would have perhaps changed his life and made him the face of the biggest basketball shoe and apparel company on Earth.

After Spencer's All-NBA season in 1972–73, a representative from a growing sneaker company based in Portland approached him about a partnership. In the early 1970s, the basketball-shoe game was dominated by Converse, which had transformed its Chuck Taylor shoe into more modern footwear for the demands of the more athletic player; Adidas, which began as a wildly popular shoe for track-and-field athletes; and Puma, which was Adidas' primary competitor in non-basketball athletic shoes and was becoming more popular with NBA players.

Nike wasn't part of that mass popularity quite yet, but it was seeking a spokesman, and the 24-year-old Spencer, one of the league's rising stars, was tops on its list.

"We were up in the Northwest, like Portland, Seattle, and Nike was just like, 'Let's break out of this area here and we need this superstar to do it,'" he said. "And I was All-NBA first-team. So they came to me and basically said, 'Let's do this deal and you can write your own ticket.'"

At an impromptu meeting at Seattle University, Nike representatives told Spencer he was their man. It was the early days of shoe endorsements, nothing close to the $100 million deals players such as LeBron James and Zion Williamson signed when entering the NBA.

"It was '73 now, he hadn't had the company set up yet. So I was like, 'Okay, I'm down with this new shoe company,'" he said. "Adidas was paying a little bit and I wore Converse, but Converse was killing my feet. That was because of John McLendon and John was with Converse all those years and I was trying to be loyal. When Nike came around I was like, 'Just work out the deal, guys.'"

Nike didn't have a lot of cash or a lucrative contract offer to make because it was a growing company (less than 10 years old), but it did offer Spencer stock—a chance to be an investor in the swoosh.

"The number that I remember... [was] 10 percent of the stock. In talking with Nike [later], everybody said, 'Nah we didn't offer you that much,'" Spencer said. "But I had some stock. And I do know my agent couldn't figure out how he got paid out of the stock, because he was a hustler and [stock didn't do anything for him.]"

Spencer did not want to reveal the name of the agent, but he said the agent was consumed with how he was going to be paid by such a Nike deal. A deal that included company stock would not result in cash assets for the agent.

Spencer also made the mistake of signing a power of attorney to that agent, who agreed to accept a $100,000 payment for his client (the equivalent of nearly $600,000 in 2020) for the endorsement opportunity. The agent then took the stock and sold it to liquidate the returns.

It was a mistake that would haunt Spencer.

"I'm on the road and we went through all types of business transactions," Spencer said. "So he had my power of attorney because we were doing transaction on top of transaction. He came back and he sold my stock and he said, 'You need to take the money now because it's gonna dry up,' and all along and we're trying to keep my salary at a place where I wouldn't have to pay so much taxes, so we didn't want to drive up the revenue."

Spencer said he brought Iman into the equation to help galvanize the Nike team in the 1970s, organizing a party in Sun Valley, Idaho, with the Nike clients and their wives. Phil Knight credits Spencer with boosting his infant company in the 1970s. And, of course, Nike grew exponentially into the 1980s, when Knight was able to acquire a North Carolina rookie named Michael Jordan.

"We're going to take the cash—cash it out now," Spencer's agent told him. "You done did the job for them."

Spencer stayed a member of the Nike family for years, but he never regained that stock.

"Phil was very loyal to me for what I did," he said. "He didn't give me back my stock, but I was still a member of the Nike club."

Understandably, NBA players didn't think about shoe endorsements as massive earning engines nearly 50 years ago. Shoe companies were still 20 years from dominating the basketball business.

"We didn't think about gym shoes back then as a cash cow," he said. "'What is he talking about?' And you know what I did with that money? I had to get me a new Mercedes. I feel so stupid."

Spencer was a young player who made an immature, shortsighted decision.

"I didn't pay attention to the paperwork because I was balling. I was a young dude and I had a bunch of court cases," he said. "I just wanted to play and enjoy the game. So I had a novice looking at the contract and what he was thinking about was, 'I don't care how much they pay you, I gotta get my 10 percent.' So it made no sense to him. I wasn't watching [the] store when they said, 'We'll give you a little percentage of the company because we don't have the funds to pay for those endorsements like that.' He was just so insistent upon, 'I gotta get paid, so let's take the money.'"

Spencer claims his agent told him that he didn't want to generate too much income for his client for fear of paying more income taxes.

"But in this case, he wanted to get paid," he said.

Spencer wants to dispel the rumors that it was a billion-dollar mistake. But he admits that his agent's selfishness cost him several million dollars.

"The deal was nowhere near no billions of dollars," he said. "It was embellished. I didn't lose no billions of dollars, but I would have been a pretty rich dude. He had the power of attorney that I had signed over to him because I couldn't travel and do all of the work, so [I felt I] had to give him the power of attorney. While I was on the road, he just renegotiated and got his money."

Spencer said he enjoyed wearing Nikes and did embrace being the face of company. Eventually Nike would sign several of Spencer's contemporaries, including Moses Malone, Maurice Lucas, Norm Nixon, Artis Gilmore, Dennis Johnson, George Gervin, and Elvin Hayes. And the company also began popularizing posters that advertised their biggest clients wearing Nikes. In 1984, Nike introduced the Air Jordan shoes, taking the company into unprecedented heights.

"People were saying, 'That ain't nothing but an upside-down Newport Cigarettes logo,'" Spencer said. "It was wild times. I just didn't know. I really didn't know. Michael Jordan will call me and we'll go out to dinner and he just beats me up with that shit. If you know Michael, he's going to beat you up about something, and when we hang out he'll give me a hard time about the Nike stuff.

"But he gives me big respect too."

11

NEW YORK, NEW YORK

SPENCER WAS ONLY **26** at the end of that 1974–75 season. That's when most NBA players enter their prime. But Spencer was also considered a high-scoring player who wasn't necessarily a winning player. While that title was unfair, Spencer's star power had faded.

Spencer didn't report to Sonics' training camp as he awaited a trade. Finally, Bill Russell sent him to the New York Knicks for first-round pick Gene Short and a 1979 first-round pick, which was mere peanuts for a four-time All-Star.

"Spencer has got to be considered a superstar of the game," Knicks coach Red Holzman told the *New York Times* after the trade. "The fact that he has been around so long and is still so young and has accomplished so much is a hell of a positive note. He'll make us a lot stronger. We're getting a hell of a runner, shooter, and rebounder."

The only issue was that Spencer was coming to a team that was running on fumes after winning titles in 1970 and 1973. Eight players on the Knicks roster were older than Spencer, including Walt Frazier and Earl Monroe, Hall of Fame guards who were on the downside of their careers.

Spencer was acquired to boost the franchise back to championship contention.

"They were getting old," he said. "And the funny thing about it is, Willis Reed had retired, Jerry Lucas retired, [then] Dave DeBusschere retired. I'm gonna replace three guys? The Knicks weren't doing well and they had been champions, so when you walk in there it's like the lingering of the champions. But the fans were just coming out of loyalty, not really like we're going to do something [special]—me, Walt Frazier. It wasn't like that.

"And when those guys left, all hell broke loose. 'You bums! What the hell? You guys stink for high hell!'"

It was the final days of a great Knicks run. Spencer roomed with Phil Jackson and Bill Bradley, both of whom had major post-NBA aspirations, and Bradley spent his final season writing his memoirs. So while Spencer was entering his prime, his teammates were planning for their lives after basketball, and the difference in approach was apparent.

"I'm like, 'What the hell? These guys are retired,'" Spencer said. "Earl done had foot surgeries and Walt was getting into his broadcasting—he had that that thesaurus everywhere he went. I'm like, 'We're trying to read plays; he's learning new words.'"

The Knicks had long lost their grip on the Eastern Conference. The Boston Celtics had resurged after Russell's retirement, with Dave Cowens, John Havlicek, and Jo Jo White, and won the title in 1974. The Washington Bullets, with Elvin Hayes, Wes Unseld, and Phil Chenier, were a new power.

New York, with the aging Holzman as coach and bunch of thirty-somethings, were just trying to keep up. So again Spencer was placed in a situation where he was tabbed as the young savior but never really had a legitimate chance to win.

On one night before a game, Spencer drove his new Rolls Royce to Madison Square Garden and the parking attendant looked at him and said, "We don't have insurance for this shit. You gotta take it back home."

Because of Manhattan traffic, Spencer's only recourse was to take the subway back to the arena, donning his Knicks gym bag.

"I kept trying to find places to park my car and I couldn't because they didn't want to be liable for the thing," he said. "You could imagine what the fans were saying to me on that subway ride."

One caveat for Spencer that stemmed from the trade was a chance to live in the most bustling city in America during his physical peak. For years, Spencer had been all about ball. He never really cultivated any other interests. But now, 26 and surrounded by so many attractions, sites, and beautiful people, Spencer decided to explore his new home, taking a large big out of the city.

"Man, it was beautiful, I lived in the Liberation Bookstore, right where Malcolm [X] made his speech," he said. "I used to eat all of my meals at the Nation of Islam on 125th street. I used to get my haircut there."

It wasn't that basketball was no longer important, but Spencer figured he might as well try to enjoy his off-court life, as a young single man living in Manhattan. Spencer hit the streets, hanging in jazz clubs, attending fashion premiers and live performances. He recalls catching a young Whoopi Goldberg and was impressed with her one-woman show.

During his third season in New York, Spencer was dining at Cleo's Restaurant at 64th and Broadway, waiting to meet a blind date. Spencer dated and enjoyed himself during his time in Seattle, but had not been in a serious relationship. That soon would change.

Spencer lived right upstairs from the restaurant, in the same massive tower as famous New Yorkers such as musician Nina Simone, journalist Susan Taylor, and evangelist Reverend Ike. So he simply took the elevator down to the lobby and walked into the restaurant for the date.

Spencer's blind date brought her roommate along on the date for support, a shy 20-year-old girl who donned a hijab. Spencer talked to both of them over dinner and when the roommate lifted her head, he saw a striking woman with olive skin and breathtaking features.

He invited the blind date and her roommate to his apartment in the same building, and the roommate appeared impressed with Spencer's African art collection, as well as the Quran sitting on the coffee table. The two made a connection.

"She started reading my Quran in Arabic and I was like, 'Wow,'" he said. "So I forgot about the girl I was meeting originally and she got up, 'Y'all don't want me around, anyway.'"

So Spencer and the roommate continued the date and talked Quran, life in America, and their different backgrounds. They reconnected the next day and walked through Central Park.

The roommate was an aspiring model who went by the name Iman, although her given name was Zara Mohamed Abdulmajid. She was born in 1955 in Somalia and she spent most of her childhood in Egypt before her father moved the family back to her native country. Political unrest forced the family to move to Nairobi, where Iman attended college and modeled part time before being discovered by photographer Peter Beard, who encouraged her to move to New York.

She had already been married, but that courtship ended when she decided to move to the United States. Spencer was fascinated with Iman's intelligence and sophistication and enamored with her beauty.

"So here we have two country people—Somalia is not that big and I'm from Mississippi," he said. "I didn't have nobody and she didn't have nobody so we just clung to each other.

"And she didn't know basketball for shit."

Finally, Spencer met someone who wanted nothing from him besides affection, who didn't have any idea of his basketball journey, the Supreme Court case, or his All-Star accolades. Someone appreciated Spencer for something other than his basketball prowess, and he liked the feeling of being lauded for heart and kindness.

"She didn't know what I did, or why would they pay people to play basketball," he said. "And I asked her, 'Why would they pay people to model?' So that's why we had each other."

It was then that Spencer embraced New York's cultural world. He and Iman visited museums and concerts, fashion shows, and art galleries. His primary focus shifted from scoring points for the Knicks to pursuing this love affair. They would eventually marry in a small ceremony in 1977.

"We didn't need nobody else," he said. "And we loved hard and deep."

On the court, Spencer transformed into more of a role player for the Knicks, who were mired in mediocrity. He was the team's second-leading scorer at 19.9 points per game, the lowest output of his career. And those numbers decreased in each of the next two seasons, as Holzman retired and gave the job to Willis Reed.

The Knicks kept pushing to compete and they acquired high-scoring forward Bob McAdoo in December of 1976 from the Buffalo Braves. McAdoo was similar to Spencer in his scoring skills, but the Knicks missed the playoffs.

A team with five future Hall of Famers—Spencer, McAdoo, Frazier, Monroe, and Bradley—managed to win just 40 games in that 1976–77 season.

"We wasn't working as hard on defense," Haywood said. "Red [Holzman] was done. He didn't want to coach no more. In terms of really working on our defensive strategy? Nah. Just roll them out there and just let them play."

The issue for Spencer was he and McAdoo played the same position, and the 6-foot-10 McAdoo even played center in some of his previous stops. But that wasn't the case with the Knicks.

"We were bringing players in left and right," Spencer said. "We'd bring Lonnie Shelton in. We'd bring Bob McAdoo in. We're all playing the same position. So we're deciding who's going to play center, who's going to play small forward, who's going to play big forward. And I was the guy who had more flexibility in my game, so I'll play small forward. I'm just making adjustments for everybody and you get lost in your own game when you start making all of those adjustments. I was way out of sorts, but somebody had to make the sacrifice."

Spencer said he still enjoyed the game, but it was difficult playing an undersized power forward against the behemoths of the 1970s that included gold-toothed Gus Johnson and the burly Wes Unseld.

"Those were men. So I had to bring my big-boy drawers then," he said. "We go down to Portland, me and Maurice Lucas had some good battles. But I'll tell you who was the dude nobody gives credit to is Sidney Wicks."

(Wicks, like Spencer, experienced drug issues during his career after a brilliant start as a rookie with the Portland Trail Blazers. Wicks eventually became a part of one of the most lopsided trades in league history, when the Celtics shipped him to the Clippers for a deal that included Tiny Archibald and a second-round pick that eventually became Danny Ainge.)

Speaking of McAdoo, Spencer said he was excited about hanging with his buddy once McAdoo came to the Knicks. But McAdoo decided to live in New Jersey and the two never really connected off the floor, which sent Spencer further into the New York party and fashion scene.

In 1976–77, Spencer experienced his first major injury as a basketball player, tearing the medial collateral ligament in his right knee, an injury he played with throughout that season, before missing two months during the Knicks' push for the playoffs. His scoring dropped to a career-low 16.5 points per game and he felt less and less wanted by the Knicks.

"I never had a chance to heal," said Spencer, who said the club didn't allow him to fully recover from early season surgery. "One leg was in a cast up to my thigh and then when I played, one leg was bigger than the other."

For Spencer, he hadn't lost his love for the game, but he gained love for other aspects of life. And that wasn't lost on him.

"It was a relief," he said. "It's kind of weird, you know? Because I kind of let it slip. It was like I needed a break from basketball. Basketball had brought me so much pain and it was just different. I immersed myself into that lifestyle, as opposed to being in the gym, working hard, and [Iman] didn't understand it, so she was trying to make me feel comfortable and I would tell her the stories about all the players that are here because of me but they hate me."

Spencer said he never stopped feeling disdain from his NBA brethren, despite the fact that players such as Moses Malone, George Gervin, and Bill Willoughby had entered the NBA or ABA straight out of high school, or without finishing their college eligibility in Gervin's case.

And ironically, just months after Spencer's verdict prevented the NBA from disallowing players who had not finished their college eligibility, the league instituted a hardship draft. The September 1971 draft, for the first time, enabled teams to choose players who wanted to enter the draft with college eligibility remaining. The penalty was that the NBA team had to forfeit their first-round pick in next year's draft.

The Washington Bullets took Phil Chenier with their hardship draft pick, and he helped the club win a championship in 1978. It was a further testament to how much Spencer had changed the game, but he still felt like he was considered an outcast for changing the system.

"That never went away," he said. "That never happened until I entered the Hall of Fame. And people got a chance to see who I am, because people didn't know who I was. They thought I was a mean, radical person, and I never was that person. I was living up to that

The first picture ever taken of Spencer. Notice the black eye. Spencer says his brother Andrew, annoyed that Spencer was getting a photo when he had not the previous year, gave it to him on purpose.

Spencer's mother, Eunice, at the sewing machine, where all the family's clothes were made.

Spencer's father, John.

Spencer and Will Robinson in the Olympic Village at the 1968 Mexico City Olympics. Spencer says this is the moment when Robinson told him, "I will kill you if you do anything like what Tommie Smith and John Carlos did." *(AP Images)*

Spencer dominating Yugoslavia in the gold-medal game on October 25, 1968. *(Bettmann / Contributor, Getty Images)*

Spencer at the University of Detroit, where he was an All-American and the Outstanding College Player of the Year. *(AP Images)*

Spencer receives the 1969–1970 ABA Most Valuable Player Award—a season in which he was also Rookie of the Year. *(Bettmann / Contributor, Getty Images)*

Into the open arms of the ABA. Here, Spencer Haywood drives around Craig Raymond of the Los Angeles Stars in an ABA playoff game while with the Denver Rockets. *(AP Images)*

Spencer leaves U.S. district court in Los Angeles with attorney Al Ross (left) and president of the Seattle SuperSonics Sam Schulman (middle) on January 8, 1971, after a ruling that permitted Spencer to resume play with the SuperSonics.
(AP Images / Wally Fong)

Spencer drains a jump shot during a 1971 game between the Sonics and the 76ers.
(Bettmann / Contributor, Getty Images)

Spencer in the first-ever basketball ad by Nike.

New York brought a lot of changes. Here, Spencer DJs during the 3:00–5:00 PM slot at the WRVR jazz station in 1976. *(Carlos Rene Perez)*

Spencer; Iman; and their daughter, Zulekha, on the cover of *Essence* magazine.

Spencer shooting over Larry Bird with the Lakers in a 1980 game in Boston. *(Focus on Sport / Getty Images)*

Piazza San Marco in Venice. Welcome to Italy, Spencer.

The Spencer Heywood Rule would go on to change the careers of so many future stars, including Michael Jordan, who left North Carolina after his junior season . . .

. . . and Kobe Bryant, who went to the NBA straight from high school.

Spencer shows off his 1968 Olympic gold medal to the kids during an NBA Cares event.

Hall of Famer Nancy Lieberman, Spencer, Hall of Famer Dan Issel, and David Stern, Spencer's biggest supporter after his playing career.

Spencer is presented with a framed jersey at his SuperSonics jersey retirement ceremony during halftime of a 2007 game (which the Sonics would go on to win by exactly 24 points). *(AP Photo/Ron Wurzer)*

Spencer finally got the call from the Hall of Fame in 2015. Here he is with the rest of that year's class. From left: Spencer, George Raveling, John Calipari, Dick Bavetta, Louie Dampier, Dikembe Mutumbo, and (Spencer's '68 Olympic teammate) Jo Jo White. *(AP Photo/Charlie Neibergall)*

Spencer and his wife of 30 years, Linda, at the wedding of Spencer's daughter, Dr. Shaakira Heywood-Stewart. (In the background, Thurgood Marshall can be seen still looking over Spencer's shoulder.)

Spencer's two youngest daughters, Shaakira and Isis.

Spencer is spending his years trying to help the younger generations. Here he is with Kevin Durant during his tenure as chairman of the Retired Players Association.

And discussing how the official name of the "early entry" rule should be the "Spencer Haywood Rule" with two beneficiaries of it, Carmelo Anthony (one year at Syracuse) and LeBron James (straight from high school).

Spencer's daughter Courtney (holding his grandson, Spencer); his wife, Linda; daughter Isis (graduating college); Spencer; and his daughter Shaakira.

person, but I'm not him. And I felt so out of my skin. I was just walking in somebody else's skin.

"I'm walking around like I'm Malcolm X, but I'm Spencer. I didn't like this shit. It's sort of like what [Colin] Kaepernick is doing [now]. But I wanted to play."

Spencer's production continued to decrease during his final years in New York. A man who had averaged 30 points per game in the ABA and 29 during his best season in Seattle managed just one 30-point game during the 1977–78 season.

By then the Knicks had traded Frazier to the Cleveland Cavaliers, sending a franchise legend to the basketball version of Siberia. The Knicks reached the playoffs under Reed, with Spencer now a secondary-scoring option, but they were swept by Julius Erving and the Philadelphia 76ers in the Eastern Conference semifinals. (The Knicks wouldn't advance beyond that point for another 15 years.)

"You know one thing about the Knicks, I never went to anybody's home—the coaches, the players, no one," he said. "Because in Seattle, you hung out together all the time. I only went to one person's house, and that was Earl Monroe. That was some strange shit to me.

"They were business. They were like a corporation, like professional. I don't like this professional shit. I like balling. They were business."

Spencer said he never felt quite comfortable in New York. During times when he was practicing or working out at the Garden, he couldn't put in a couple of extra hours without being kicked out by arena officials because they had to prepare for another event.

Halfway through the next season, the Knicks shipped Spencer to the New Orleans Jazz for Joe C. Meriweather. It was a trade that served as a blessing and a curse for Spencer.

"I wanted out," Spencer said of New York. "I didn't want to leave my wife, but I just had a bad experience in New York. The press was very mean towards me. There were a lot of lies spread out about me—I was lazy and didn't want to work. But hell, I was in love. Check my shit out. I was trying to live another life. I hadn't had another life.

"It just wasn't my kind of ball."

While Spencer had the freedom in Seattle, but was eventually resented for being the star, he could never find that comfort in New York. The Knicks shuffled players in and out, trying to find past glory. It failed miserably.

"It was cool playing for Red [Holzman], but he kept trying to make me into Dave DeBusschere, Willis Reed, and Jerry Lucas. And I said to Red, 'But I kicked all their asses, why would I want to be them?' And the media would beat me down because I had another life and I embraced my life with my wife and her crew of people. They didn't know me for basketball—like Calvin Klein and those people—they knew me as Spencer, this decent person, and I had acceptance.

"Everybody thought I was being snooty and the Knicks players [were saying], 'He's too good for us.' We didn't even look at ourselves like that. That was same bad shit."

In the 2017 HBO series *The Deuce*, about the New York porn and prostitution scene in the 1970s, "Frankie," played by James Franco, walked into an X-rated movie theater and asked Mario the bouncer about the Knicks.

"You catch the Knicks game last night?" Frankie asks Mario.

"Aw, man," Mario says.

"McAdoo, right? Now we gotta get Spencer in order and we got something," Frankie says. "Should have at least covered the spread... Spencer killed me in the second half—killed me. And that's what you get for dating a fashion model! How you gonna focus when you got that... banging around in your head? It's impossible! You can't do it!"

"To this day, I say Goddamn, you still beating on me?" Spencer said. "New York is very hard if you aren't winning, but it's also hard when you're looking to be different. They sold me as this savior coming to New York to save the Knicks and now I got this outside life.

"The New York fans were so mean to me and to my wife. She'd come to a game and be cheering out of order because she had never seen basketball. She was a star and they would be messing with her."

And Spencer also thought he was being discriminated against because he was in a relationship with an African woman.

"You gotta remember, I married a foreigner, like my mother said," Spencer said. "People looked at Somalia at that time… like pro-Russia [Communist] and unexpectedly I was in some shit and I was like, 'We ain't even into no politics.'"

Spencer said he made a mistake by going on *Good Morning America* with Iman during that time, telling the host he wanted to bring more advanced technology to Africa while bringing more African culture to the United States.

"You gotta think back to that period and we didn't understand our power," he said.

By the late 1970s Somalia was being governed by a socialist party with ties to the Soviet Union, at the height of the Cold War.

"We were two powerful people but we never looked at our power like that," Spencer said. "We were just two lovebirds."

In 1978, Iman and Spencer had their only child, a daughter named Zulekha. And soon after, Iman's modeling career ascended, making her a superstar.

"We didn't have anybody," Spencer said. "We just had each other. Of course, when I married her, I brought her Somalian family over to my home and they lived with me. That was my crew.

"And honestly, I just wanted to get her home every night."

12

NOT FOR LONG

S PENCER NEEDED TO GET OUT of New York. The off-court distractions were derailing his career. The Knicks weren't going anywhere and his role was reduced. New Orleans had gained an expansion team in 1974 and acquired former Louisiana State star Pete Maravich as its headliner.

The result was predictable. Maravich put on a nightly show but the Jazz usually lost. Again, Spencer got a chance to play for another legend in Elgin Baylor, who wanted to focus his offense around Spencer and a young, emerging power forward named Leonard "Truck" Robinson.

Iman stayed in New York while Spencer got an apartment in the French Quarter, close to the Superdome, which the Jazz shared with the NFL's Saints. Spencer lived at the Superdome, going there several times a day to get shots up. Spencer had regained his love for the game. Baylor even told him to explore the New Orleans nightlife, but Spencer had no interest.

"I'm like, 'Shit, I got good food, I got a gym to work out in any time I want to, I'm happy,'" he said. "And I wanted to put my game on the map so I put all my shit together, averaging 24 and 10 [rebounds]."

For his 34-game stint with the Jazz, Spencer looked like his old self. He averaged 25 points a game in his final 14 games with the club, returning to that prolific scorer that had thrilled fans in Seattle.

After the season, Spencer returned to New York, reinvigorated about his basketball career, ready for a full season with the Jazz. "And then I come back to New York," Spencer said, "and they're talking about the team's moving to Utah."

The Jazz's time in New Orleans was over. The Superdome was too large to host a basketball team, attendance dwindled because the team was porous, and management made the hideous decision to trade their 1979 first-round pick to the Los Angeles Lakers in 1976 for aging Gail Goodrich in an attempt to sell tickets.

Goodrich played his final three NBA seasons with the Jazz, as mostly a role player.

That No. 1 pick the Jazz gave the Lakers ended up being Earvin "Magic" Johnson.

"I didn't know Utah," Spencer said. "I can't take my wife and my family to Utah. They just got used to New York and they've been in exile. Nobody understood that. I know it's my job, I know that. But can I be some place where they can feel more comfortable?

"And Utah probably would have been the best place for me. That's where I could have went to work. I would have never gotten into this high stage."

13

THE DEVIL

SPEAKING OF THE **L**AKERS, with the 6-foot-9-inch Magic Johnson coming in, the club didn't have much need for ball-dominant forward Adrian Dantley. So they dealt the former Rookie of the Year to the new Utah Jazz for Spencer, hoping Spencer would adapt to a secondary role for a title-contending team.

New Lakers coach Jack McKinney recruited Spencer to come to the Lakers, promising to work out a deal. Meanwhile, Jazz general manager Frank Layden implored Spencer to be the face of the franchise in Utah.

"I tried to explain to Frank, 'I got a family,'" he said. "My wife has a career. Wives didn't have careers. It's hard to explain to somebody."

Abdul-Jabbar, now nearing his mid-thirties and without a title in Los Angeles, pushed for the trade. Spencer was still only 30, coming off a resurgent season with the Jazz, and had never been close to an NBA Finals. And Spencer had a chance to play with perhaps the best point guard in NBA history as he approached greatness.

"I couldn't believe it," Spencer said of Magic's talent. "You would hear people from Michigan talking about how good he was, but in training camp in Palm Springs, I was like, 'Wow.' But I loved his enthusiasm. I used to love that shit. Because it's somebody expressing what I couldn't express because I had been suppressed because if my era. You couldn't show that kind of emotion. It wasn't cool. And when I did it in Seattle, they said, 'He's a hot dog.'"

There was no reason why this wouldn't work out.

But there was, and it had nothing to do with basketball.

"While I'm there, the Devil came in," he said of his time in Los Angeles. "In the form of coke."

Spencer was not new to cocaine. It was in abundance in the 1970s, especially at some of those ritzy parties he frequented in New York. He snorted a couple of lines, took a shot of bourbon, and kept it moving. It didn't have that type of effect on him.

"I never liked it," he said. "The thing I liked was weed. I don't like no shit out of the process. That was the rule, you didn't take shit that was processed. But here I am in L.A. and some of the guys who had retired, they were in this thing to the max, and I'm hanging out with some of my Motown people [from] back in the day. Shit yeah, man, I was like, 'How did I get tricked into this shit?'"

But Spencer wasn't alone. Cocaine use plagued the NBA in the late '70s. Players such as Marvin Barnes, Micheal Ray Richardson, and John Lucas were riddled with drug issues. Cocaine had become the vogue drug in the disco-and-party-influenced '70s and many NBA players indulged, before the league had any real drug policy.

With players earning in the hundreds of thousands of dollars and cocaine promising a better and more intense high than weed, the NBA had a real problem.

"We had an 80 percent crisis in the NBA with cocaine that year," Spencer said. "Why pick me?"

Spencer said he tried cocaine before but his use after he moved to Los Angeles became a concern. The Lakers were a team with championship aspirations.

Magic was the prized rookie and seized the vocal leadership role. Abdul-Jabbar was the five-time MVP and backbone, but he didn't engage in the Los Angeles party life. He would play games and then head right up to his Bel Air mansion, smoke a joint, and read the Quran.

He said he wasn't the only one using.

On the floor, Spencer cemented himself as a reliable scoring option off the bench. At age 30, and coming off a knee injury, Spencer wasn't the dynamic scorer of the past, but he could score in spurts. The Lakers were such a deep team with Johnson, Abdul-Jabbar, rookie guard Michael Cooper, veteran Jamaal Wilkes, and scoring guard Norm Nixon.

A few weeks after the Lakers acquired Spencer from the Jazz, they added another seasoned veteran in burly forward Jim Chones, who became Abdul-Jabbar's protector and the team's enforcer. The Lakers were ready for a title run.

And despite the best chance for team success in his career, a chance to be a champion, Spencer spent most of that year in a cocaine-induced haze. The drug had him by the balls.

"That was like my missing year in life," he said. "It really was. My family being out there and I had Iman with me and my young daughter. I played all right. I came there with 24 and 10 and I had my shit right. And this thing got in my life.

"Well I'll just do it like my mom would say—the Devil. The Devil got in there, man, and it was controlling me completely and I wasn't myself. Those players never got a chance to see who Spencer Haywood is and was. Players who knew me on that team, they know me. This ain't fair."

Spencer said his cocaine use was pretty open. But there was no intervention. Spencer continued to descend without interference.

"I didn't get no help," he said. "I didn't get nobody to encourage me to, like 'Hey, man, will you stop?' It was like, 'Where you gonna be tonight, man? I'll come by late.' I thought somebody would say if you're off the rocker, 'C'mon dude.'"

Spencer said staying in Utah would have kept him off cocaine. But Los Angeles was the sinner's paradise in 1979. Folks who felt they'd achieved a certain level of success were seeking a new hobby, and there was a glamour attached to cocaine, to going to the vogue club.

"It was happening in L.A.," he said. "Everybody was doing this new thing. And it wasn't like crack, where you see the addicts on the street. Cocaine was supposed to be the clean way of not clogging up your nose.

"But I knew it was messed up the first time I really got involved in it. I knew something was really very wrong from the first night. I knew it. I knew it. I knew it."

Spencer describes scenes with his L.A. buddies where those who cooked the cocaine would walk around with chef hats on, whipping up another potent dose of nose candy. A generation before, musicians Billie Holiday, Charlie Parker, and Frankie Lymon were killing themselves with heroin use, stabbing needles into their veins to get high.

Cocaine addiction hadn't overtaken the country like it would in the mid-1980s. Getting hooked wasn't a major fear. Those who did cocaine could afford it. And soon snorting was replaced by freebasing, which was considered a cleaner way to get the high.

Once freebasing replaced snorting, and the high became more profound, Spencer was hooked.

"All of the impurities fall to the bottom and the rock floats up to the top," Spencer's cocaine-cooking buddies would tell him. "That's the purity. That's the beauty of it. It's almost like organic, man."

"Hell nah, I didn't believe that shit," Spencer said. "But I don't know what got into me. It was like this Devil and being from down South and being in the church all of my life, even though I had my time with Islam, I knew that was the Devil. So when I sit there and I smoke and I smoke and it was something about it that I couldn't leave.

"It was like four in the morning and I got practice and that's when I left. And it continued on that flight. Damn, what kind of shit is this?"

Cocaine use became Spencer's No. 1 hobby, and he pushed aside basketball and began ignoring his family.

"Iman is complaining because I'm not home," he said. "And then when I got to practice—I would get to practice on time but not really in time."

Spencer had been just happy to be on the Lakers when the season started, but the constant drug use turned him into a dark and bitter man. And the lack of practice, the drug's effect on his body, and the late nights were taking away from his game.

The Lakers were playing well, but it was under a new coach. McKinney, who recruited Spencer to Los Angeles, suffered serious injuries in a bicycle accident on November 8, 1979, an incident that would change the direction of the Lakers' franchise.

Lakers general manager Jerry West and owner Jerry Buss immediately named Paul Westhead, who joined McKinney's staff from LaSalle University, as the interim head coach. Spencer felt Westhead had something against him, and of course the cocaine use and the inconsistent playing time led to his paranoia.

And he went from singing Motown songs, playing the part of Temptations crooner David Ruffin on the team bus, to sitting surly in the back, angry that he wasn't playing and confused as to why his teammates weren't supporting him. Westhead suspended Spencer for a three-game December road trip for complaining about playing time.

He then descended into becoming a recluse.

"I run into this thing where I just read. I was alone and being alone on the bus, on the plane, I just read," he said. "I immersed myself into books... but I'm thinking, *When I get home from this flight, I gotta fire me up something.*"

The contradiction of reading James Baldwin's *The Fire Next Time* on the plane and then looking forward to his next cocaine hit wasn't lost on Spencer. He had become a human contradiction.

"What kind of insane shit is that?" he said. "I'm reading this great book and the one thing... I could think of [was] lighting up some cocaine. That was some sick shit, man. I don't have nobody to blame. That was on me.

"But I thought maybe somebody on my team—given what I had given to the game—would like turn me on to help. Help me. Pull me aside, like, 'You don't even know what you're doing. You're out to lunch, you're hanging out with these people in California, you got strangers coming to the games in your seats while your wife is out of town. What the hell?'

"I mean they told me all of that afterwards, but I was like, 'What the hell? Where were you beforehand?'"

But Spencer wasn't alone. Cocaine use was destroying the careers of rising business people, actors, and highly paid athletes.

"I seen players that would have had tremendous careers but that shit was out here, man," he said. "Everybody was doing it."

Spencer's playing time decreased as the season progressed, especially after the Lakers acquired the rugged Mark Landsberger from the Chicago Bulls in midseason and he immediately became a fan favorite. The Lakers won 60 games that season, as Westhead implemented an up-tempo offense that would make L.A. the most exciting offense in the NBA.

Johnson, with his lanky 6'9" frame, raced the ball up the floor with his long strides and then used his uncanny court vision to find open teammates for baskets. Abdul-Jabbar was rejuvenated. Wilkes was splashing 20-footers with his behind-the-head release. Cooper was the defensive stopper and Nixon was the underrated scorer. The Lakers had everything working and Spencer was relegated to hanging on for the ride.

In 74 of his 76 appearances, Spencer scored 19 points or fewer. And he averaged 8.4 points in his final 32 games of the regular season. Spencer was essentially just a guy on this roster. The same situation occurred in the playoffs, when Spencer played extensive minutes in only three games of the opening series against the Phoenix Suns, two of which were blowouts.

He played just 48 minutes in the five-game series win over the defending-champion Sonics, and then five minutes total in the first two games of the NBA Finals against the Philadelphia 76ers.

But Spencer's demise in Los Angeles culminated on the morning of May 2, two days before Game 1 of the Finals.

14

THE END AND THE BEGINNING

A NIGHT AFTER SOME HARD PARTYING, an exhausted Spencer dozed off during a routine stretching exercise during the Lakers practice at the team's facility in West Los Angeles. Cooper tried to awaken Spencer and he wouldn't budge.

Soon after his teammates surrounded him, he woke in horror. Spencer had tried his best to keep his habit private. Spencer was hung over and still high. His body had just shut down. Cocaine had taken over.

Spencer wasn't disciplined yet. The Lakers split the first two games and Spencer played a combined five minutes. Before the Lakers traveled to Philadelphia for Game 3, the team's brass of Westhead, West, and Buss met with Spencer.

He was going to be suspended for the rest of the season. They had had enough. The addiction rumors had become too loud.

"He's useless," one Laker told the *New York Times*. "He's just hopeless."

The Lakers held a press conference to announce the suspension, and Westhead didn't mention the practice incident. But it was a series of misdoings: calling Westhead a "liar," complaining about playing time, an argument with Chones and little-used reserved Brad Holland during practice, and showing up late to another practice during the playoffs.

Spencer still thought he was a star, but with the Lakers he was just another aging athlete who was now an addict. And he was the only one who didn't realize that.

"The low point was when I was expelled from the Lakers with three games to go [in the Finals]," he said. "I was trying to get back because at least I'll go to the ring ceremony and participate in the parade, but when they snatched that away from me and I was like, 'Wow, shit.'"

The Lakers played hardball with Spencer. Not only was he banned from participating in the parade after the Lakers beat the 76ers in six games—punctuated by Johnson's 42-point, 15-rebound, seven-assist masterpiece in Game 6—he was given only a third of the playoff share.

What's more, the Lakers essentially played six players during the last four games of the Finals, meaning there would have been a possible role for Spencer.

The Lakers also denied Spencer a championship ring (he got one years later). It was like the organization tried its best to remove any memory of him from the Lakers' first championship in eight years. He had brought embarrassment to the franchise, and he paid a dear price.

"They were giving championship rings to [actor] Lou Gossett," he said. "They were giving playoff shares to Jack Curran, the trainer. Is this a low blow or what? It was a hostile environment. Everybody wanted to get [my issues] off their shoulders, not just the Lakers. The league wanted to get it off, so we can wrap it around one person, expel them from the league."

Spencer was still under contract with the Lakers, and he said he lobbied to be exposed in the expansion draft so he could play with the new Dallas Mavericks, which were beginning play in the 1980–81 season with new coach Dick Motta.

Spencer was convinced the league wanted to make an example out of him, and why would the Lakers do Spencer a favor by allowing him to play for an expansion team where he would most immediately become its best player.

He said the NBA informed him after that 1980 season that the only way he would collect the remainder of his Lakers' contract was to sign with Carrera Venezia of the Italian League. In the early 1980s, Europe was a haven for aging NBA players or high draft picks who failed and were looking to continue to their careers.

Spencer is convinced the NBA, still smarting from the Supreme Court case from a decade before, wanted to punish him, and also wanted to create the perception it was ridding the league of drug-using players.

"I got word that I gotta go," he said. "I didn't get a chance to solicit to another team or anything. Dr. [Ernie] Vandeweghe [father of NBA executive and retired player Kiki] spent a lot of time with me during that stretch and the word he got from my agent is that you gotta go."

The risk of Spencer seeking other work in the NBA was having his Lakers contract voided, and he still felt as if many owners held a grudge from the court case. There was no guarantee the Mavericks, or any other NBA team, would sign him, especially after rumors of his heavy drug use surfaced.

"Everybody was trying to wrap everything up in 1980, like this [drug] thing never existed," he said. "The one guy that did it was this guy. I wasn't allowed to go to Dallas in the expansion. They got me out of town during that summer. [Said] 'You've got to go to Venice to receive your contract from the Lakers.'"

On a clip from 2010 HBO documentary: *Magic & Bird: A Courtship of Rivals*, a highlight of Spencer on the Sonics is shown as the narrator described the heavy drug use when Johnson and Bird entered the league in 1979.

He believes the league tried to use him as an example for years.

"And the one player they showed, of all the players in the league, they had my jersey on my back," he said. "They kept that going on for a while, that was the problem of the league. Of course, now you document and read about things and they acknowledged they had an 80 percent crisis. But I was the perfect guy because they called it the so-called 'fast lane' because I was married to a model. I had another life other than just basketball.

"I fit the character that was built, Hollywood style."

Spencer admits he fell asleep in practice. He freely admits he was high. But he also felt there were powers in the NBA who were enjoying his demise because he made such a commotion about entering the league.

"That's a hell of a penalty to place upon a person that played all of the games, did all of the practices," Spencer said. "When it came time to get through Seattle, they said, 'You gotta play 30 minutes a game.'

Because we couldn't get past Seattle into the championship [before]. We couldn't get it unless they had me at full throttle.

"And then we got Philadelphia coming up and they go, 'Aww, you don't really count.' And actually I didn't count.

"But the blame was on me because I put myself in that position and I never—my character, my life, I was never supposed to be put in that position. I had went to the Supreme Court, I went through all of this shit throughout my life and I always knew that the Big Eye is on me and I knew I couldn't mess up.

"And I did mess up, and the Big Eye got me."

Spencer was banned from the parade, even though he thought his suspension was just for the rest of the playoffs.

"They didn't look at me like I got this sickness," he said. "They looked at me like, 'We finally got this bastard down and we're going to put our hands right on his neck and choke him out.'"

Spencer said he'll never reveal the Lakers players he got high with and he accepted full blame for the situation, despite his actions during that time.

"But let me get this straight, with the Lakers, that was my responsibility. I messed that up," he said. "So I don't wanna be pointing fingers [just because] I got high with a lot of guys. But I don't want them to feel like I'm going to spill some shit. That's not my makeup. I messed up. If I had stayed straight, I wouldn't have had any of that shit."

The Lakers celebrated their first title since 1972 in grand style. And they rewarded some of their diehard celebrity fans with honorary rings, thanks to Buss.

"That's a bitter taste there, when you're handing out stuff to everybody and I played all these games, the whole season, at least give me my shit," he said. "You know I would have had six championships by now, had I stayed with the Lakers. Playing with Magic and Kareem, I had worked hard in basketball, but to play with those two guys was so easy. All I had to do is go to the other side. And Kareem shoots 70 percent on that hook shot.

"And when I was running the floor the ball was just in my hands from passes from Magic. This was some easy shit."

Spencer also claimed the players' wives resented Iman because she would arrive late to games at the Inglewood Forum. He said she didn't know how to drive and would ride with his buddy Vern DeSilva, who was a professor at Cal State Long Beach and could only come after his final class.

"It was friction and all they had to do was talk to her," he said. "She didn't know how to drive. She was from New York."

He said the jealousy of his relationship with Iman and also her celebrity caused dissension in the locker room. By this time, Iman was a rising star, and Spencer was rapidly losing his star power.

"We were country folks, we were the Beverly Hillbillies," he said. "We weren't big timers. We were Mississippi and Somalia."

Spencer recalls when he and Muhammad Ali were on *The Phil Donahue Show* because they were married to supermodels. Ali married model Veronica Porche in 1977, towards the end of his career.

"'Y'all are married to those old has-been athletes,'" Spencer said they were saying. "It was like the audience thought we were these washed-up athletes married to these supermodels. 'What the hell y'all doing married to them?'"

The hits kept coming from every direction.

15

THE KING OF ITALY

SPENCER WAS WAIVED BY THE LAKERS in August 1980, just three months after the Lakers won the NBA championship. The only way he would be able to collect on the remaining year on his deal was to play for Carrera Venezia, an Italian team based in Venice.

Spencer knew it was time for a change. The NBA was essentially kicking him out and his marriage was deteriorating. At the time, Iman's two sisters and her cousin were living with Spencer, along with his daughter.

But Iman and Spencer were growing apart. She was traveling, modeling, and soaring, while Spencer was considered an NBA washout who blew his best chance at winning a championship.

Spencer had a choice. Continue to be a martyr and outcast in the United States, with no guarantee he would play in the NBA again, or accept his exile to Italy and try to rebuild his brand halfway across the world.

"That was the beginning of the end," Spencer said. "Because when I went to Italy, it pulled the family so far apart."

He figured if he was going to play in Italy, to a new legion of basketball fans, he might as well give them his best. And Spencer was emotionally healing. He would sit on his balcony nights after games and watch the gondoliers on the water. He needed to leave the United States, and he felt betrayed by almost everyone he'd tried to help.

Signing with Carrera Venezia was a much-needed jolt of appreciation for the sagging Haywood, who was still damaged by the Lakers suspension. On his way to Venice from Los Angeles, Spencer's flight connected in Boston, where he sat for a few hours at Logan Airport.

It was there that Spencer heard a plethora of remarks from Boston fans, reminding him of his addiction and suspension. It was time to bounce for a while.

"'Why would you get to the top of the mountain and get high?'" fans told him. "There's no reason. But I wasn't the only one on that team. I'll take my beating here. I'm going to a place like, wow as much as I have done for this league. It was like Napoleon when they exiled his ass to St. Helena. My wife was crying—Iman was just dying. She finally got it through her skull that I'm going to Italy and she's got to be over there with me."

That let Spencer know it was time to get clean, even if he needed help. Before he left for Italy, DeSilva and Lakers general manager Bill Sharman encouraged Spencer to give up cocaine. He lived with DeSilva for a few weeks, began working out vigorously, and regaining his basketball life force.

What helped Spencer during his exile to Italy was the fact that Iman was fluent in Italian and she also was able to arrange modeling sessions there.

"You're gonna be happy over here," she told him. "They're going to love you."

"But I'm not in the NBA," he responded. "I'm going to kill them [on the court] when I get back."

When he arrived at the Venice Marco Polo Airport, Spencer was spotted by the locals and immediately gained a nickname that would stay with him throughout his time there.

"It was a magnificent city with all of that history and the Italians were like, 'The Moor is back! Othello is back!'" he said. "I was like, 'What are they talking about?'"

Iman explained to Spencer that to the Italians he resembled Othello, the Shakespeare character, and Othello was a Moroccan general in the Venetian Army. Moroccans are called Moors.

"I thought to myself, 'Oh hell yeah, I'm gonna play this one. This is me,'" Spencer said. "I'm the King. I got my crown again. So I walked around in Venice [and] I played ball like a king."

In those days, European basketball was several levels behind the NBA. It would be many years before the top-notch European players migrated to the NBA. In the early 1980s, European basketball was a less physical game more focused on the perimeter.

It was a perfect for the 31-year-old Spencer. He was able to play big minutes, the team gave him a beautiful villa in Venice and he was able to stay away from the drug use and perils of life in Los Angeles. In Venice, he became a team leader, arranging team dinners after games and offering advice to younger teammates during practice.

"It was so much love," he said. "I had left a place where there was a lot of hate... and then I come to Venice where it's just love and the Italian people. Like the Italian Basketball Association said, 'We got him and we're going to treat him really nice. We're not like y'all are in the NBA.' It was a great time, plus I didn't play as much as I did in the NBA."

Meanwhile, Iman scheduled shows for Venice, Milan, and Paris so she could stay close, and Spencer would accompany her on his days off.

For the first time since his Sonics days, Spencer received appreciation and adulation on the floor and was adored off the floor. The only caveat was that he had to move away from his family. But it was a needed one-year respite.

Spencer was by far the best American player to play in Europe at that time. Generally, American players headed overseas when their NBA time had run out or they were looking for one last payday.

"The Italians knew me from the Olympics. [I was] an Olympic hero in [the] '68 Olympics, [which] was so dynamic for those people," he said. "And what I did in the NBA for my first seven years, it was like, 'Wow, we got him?' It was beautiful, man, because I had so much anger. I wanted to talk about the NBA [drug issues] because we had an 80 percent crisis at that time. I mean, all the people that I sit around the table getting high with, they turned on me. So I was angry."

Spencer decided he wanted to take notes about his pain and anger. Iman got ahold of those notes and told him that harboring so much resentment wasn't healthy and wouldn't help him get clean. Iman tore up those notes.

As for his personal life, that was suffering. He and Iman were growing apart. While they had a daughter to take care of, Spencer was still trying to find happiness and deal with the bitterness.

"I'm Christian and she's a Muslim and we started praying together as Muslims and we started praying together as Christians," he said. "So we started praying away all this evil shit that happened because those people in L.A. were her dear friends."

Spencer knew he was still good enough to play in the NBA, not ready to be cast off to Europe to keep playing professional basketball for a couple of extra bucks. But it was a necessary move.

He would take a water taxi from his apartment off the water to the arena. And the fans would be waiting for him to arrive every night chanting, "*Grande Haywood! Grande Haywood!*"

"I needed to feel the love again and Italy was the perfect place," he said. "I was clean and finally completely healthy. I had my game together and all I had to do was just play ball. Everything else was taken care of.

"It was awesome that first game, and boy did I lay it out there. I was ready. I had been working out. I was in shape. I was like, *I might be here in Italy, but I'm gonna make you cry, make you want me bad in the NBA.* I couldn't wait to get back to America."

In Carrera Venezia's opener against rival Turisanda, Haywood was matched up against old NBA rival Tim Bassett, who played with the New York/New Jersey Nets. Bassett, who had been waived earlier in the year by the San Antonio Spurs after just five games, was exactly the type of NBA player who migrated to Europe.

"Tim was like, 'Goddamn, boy, you got your shit. You are balling, man,'" Spencer said. "Tim said, 'Nah, man, you don't belong over here. But you should stay over here because you're making it better for all of us.' It just went on like that that whole year."

When Carrera Venezia's games were broadcast on Italian national television, Iman got a chance to see a rejuvenated Spencer in action.

"She didn't see my balling skills before," he said. "When she was in Italy, I dropped 50, 25 boards, seven assists. It was like, 'Who is this dude that I'm married to here?' Everybody in the whole country is calling me, 'Champion! Champion! Spencer Haywood.' It gave them life, it gave them party, the Italian Basketball Association. 'You may have Kareem, but we have Spencer.'"

He played with Yugoslavian standout Drazen Dalipagic, a three-time Olympic medalist and FIBA World Cup MVP, and 2004 Naismith Hall of Fame enshrinee under legendary Italian coach Tonino Zorzi.

"We were balling man, and they wasn't giving anything to me because I went and got it," he said. "I was doing about 17 boards and seven offensive a game. So I was going to get that shit, like picking cotton again. It was hard work."

During his Italian season, Lakers general manager Bill Sharman came over to Venice and visited Spencer, telling him that moving on from the Lakers situation and suppressing the anger would be the best path back to the league.

He had been essentially kicked out of the NBA, he felt the league made him a scapegoat. He was the most accomplished player that was diagnosed with a serious drug problem, and the NBA had an identity crisis.

The NBA was losing fans, it was theorized, because the league was too Black, something those owners who sought to prevent Spencer and his teenage brethren from entering the league surely believed. But they couldn't stop the tide. The NBA was dominated by Black players and during a time when money became plentiful and the lifestyle lavish, Spencer and some of his cohorts indulged.

Spencer was having trouble getting past his anger at Westhead. As usual, it was Eunice who helped alter his mindset. After a phone call to Eunice, who calmed him and instructed him to focus on the future, he decided to put his attention squarely where he was.

Italy was utopia, but eventually Spencer knew he was going to have to come back and face his fears and obstacles.

The NBA was always calling. Scouts began making themselves present at Carrera Venezia games the second half of the season. Spencer still had something left, but needed to show he was ready to return. So executives from the Washington Bullets began calling. They were looking for a small forward to make another playoff push.

"I was having a tremendous year and everybody was coming over and saying, 'Shit, this is a different ballplayer,'" he said.

General manager Bob Ferry (whose son Danny would enjoy a 13-year NBA career) called Spencer to reassure him that another chance to play in the NBA wouldn't result in betrayal. Spencer also had conversations with Bullets coach Gene Shue, a longtime coach who faced Spencer numerous times over his career.

They told Spencer they were going to fly him from Venice to Washington, D.C., the night of their meeting. There was one catch: Spencer didn't have a passport. The owner of the Carrera Venezia had taken his passport for fear of losing him to the NBA.

However, Spencer and Iman were able to meet with management and get his passport back.

Spencer considered staying in Italy for another season because he was being paid by Carrera Venezia *and* the Lakers, as owner Jerry

Buss relented and decided to pay Haywood in addition to his Italian deal with deferred compensation.

Plus, in Italy, he was the King.

"But it wasn't about the money, it was about my joy and my peace," he said. "I was at a beautiful place and I just didn't want to be back in America where everybody is walking around like, 'Hey man, I got some shit here.' Players on opposing teams talking shit. I was not that secure about that. Because that shit did a number on me. I wasn't like all the other guys who would do the [drug] shit and it didn't bother them.

"But me? I've had family members perish because of alcoholism, so it was that gene man, that gene. So I wanted to protect myself."

Spencer had stayed clean in Italy. He did nothing stronger than weed. As one of the more famous Black men in Italy, it was hard for Spencer to cop a hit inconspicuously. So he didn't.

"I just didn't want that lifestyle," he said. "I just didn't want that shit near me."

16

TIME TO GO HOME

ON OCTOBER **24, 1981,** Spencer returned to the NBA, signing a two-year contract with the Washington Bullets. Six days later, he scored 10 points in the season opener against the Boston Celtics.

"I jumped on the plane, flew all night, hit the floor, and we were playing the Celtics," he said. "And in Washington, I came out looking like a cool Italian dude with a scarf around my neck. I had on all my leather and the rest of the guys were like, 'What the hell?'"

But Spencer was scared. He still didn't trust the NBA. A return is what he wanted, but he thought maybe the league had a more elaborate plan to further embarrass him.

"I was really nervous about going back to the NBA, because I thought they may put some shit [drugs] in my bag," he said. "I had some good conversations with Bob Ferry and Gene Shue. I knew it was time to come back."

The Bullets won the NBA title in 1978 but only had residue from that team. They needed Spencer just as much as he needed them.

While Iman and his family remained in New York, Haywood purchased a condo in Chevy Chase, Maryland, about 21 miles from the Capital Centre in Landover.

It began slowly for Spencer. The Bullets started the season 4–11 and Spencer played a secondary role off the bench. Eventually he worked his way into the starting lineup and the Bullets made a furious run towards the playoffs, winning 12 of their final 18 games.

"The first season, man I was balling," he said. "And we made that big playoff run. Basketball was fun again. I still had some magic left and it was good for me, because Iman and the family would come hang out with me every weekend.

In that stretch, Spencer averaged 18 points and six rebounds, including a 27-point game against the New Jersey Nets and a 25-point effort against the Chicago Bulls. Spencer wasn't what he once was, but he still had some game.

After the Bullets beat the Nets in the first-round miniseries, they matched up with the defending champion Celtics in the second round. For Spencer, he experienced a renaissance.

While the Bullets had little chance of beating a team with four Hall of Famers—Larry Bird, Kevin McHale, Robert Parish, and Nate Archibald—Spencer used the series as a personal showcase.

He averaged 22.2 points and 5.6 rebounds in the five-game set. In his second-to-last career appearance at the Boston Garden, Spencer scored 26 points in Game 2 in a 103–102 win.

The basketball-savvy Celtics fans appreciated Spencer's efforts in that Game 2 by giving him an ovation during his performance. It was a verification of his skills and a sign of acceptance after feeling like an outcast for so many years.

"The Celtics fans gave me so much love when I came back," he said. "The Celtics fans, they relate to basketball, they stood up and cheered so much like, 'Wow, this guy's been shitted on so badly by the Lakers. So we're going to give him big respect.' So that was a beautiful thing."

The second season in Washington did not work out so well. Spencer got into a collision during the preseason with Philadelphia's Darryl Dawkins and strained his calf. While he was injured, Spencer decided to try a hit of cocaine again. And a second hit followed the first hit.

Meanwhile, Spencer struggled on the floor. After a loss at Philadelphia in which he went 6 for 16 from the field, Spencer was heavily criticized by Gene Shue to the media. The next day, November 15, Spencer met with Shue and decided he wanted to take a break from the team, feeling like he was holding the club back. He was placed on the injured-retired list for four weeks.

Eventually Spencer and the team would agree for him to return and he again became a starter. But his play declined considerably. Over a 27-game stretch, he averaged just 8.1 points and shot 39 percent from the field, far below his career averages.

On February 25, 1983, Iman was riding in a taxi cab that was blindsided by a drunk driver in Manhattan. The taxi struck a building and the force of the accident sent Iman through the windshield. She broke her cheekbone, collarbone, and ribs.

Spencer asked the Bullets to leave the team so he could care for his wife.

"Back then you couldn't go home; you couldn't take a leave of absence and say, 'Let me take care of business,'" he said. "My young daughter was there and Iman's younger sisters, Idil and Nadia, were with her in the hospital and I knew I had to go home.

They didn't have nobody to take care of them. I don't have my sisters and nobody to help and [Iman's family] had been loyal to me. So I just quit. I said, 'I'm going home man.'"

Spencer abruptly retired after playing just five minutes in a game at Denver on February 26. He missed the final 27 games of the season and Washington missed the playoffs by one game to the Atlanta Hawks. Spencer chose family over basketball and he would never play in the NBA again.

He said he regretted not sitting down with Ferry or Shue about his situation. A later conversation with Bullets assistant coach Bernie Bickerstaff revealed that he could have smoothed out the situation and preserved his reputation by just having a conversation with team management. Instead, he said he was embarrassed but felt obligated to go home. And he never regretted the decision, but it would have a major impact on his image.

"How could I tell Washington I need some time off?" he said. "They don't know my family situation—but you gotta go home. And I just quit basketball and I'll take it up with my family. Like what happened in L.A., I thought [the Bullets] were the enemy too, because I've still got that paranoia."

It took Iman five months to fully recover, but she admitted she was a different woman after the accident.

"When I thought about the fact that I wasn't dead or paralyzed, giving up my modeling career seemed a very small price to pay. I had weathered the storm; it was time to heal myself—first the physical injuries, and then the less-visible breaks," she told Oprah.com. "Recovery took five months, and I spent those long weeks reconsidering how I was going to live my life. I had to come to terms with the business of fashion and its illusions. Eventually I did go back to modeling, though I still have visible scars. After the bones mended, my left eye was smaller than my right, and my eyebrow never grew back. But you know what? Big deal. I think I became beautiful after the accident."

As life settled down following Iman's recovery, there was perhaps one last chance for Spencer Haywood: a chance to play for his hometown Detroit Pistons, a franchise on the rise with Isiah Thomas, Bill Laimbeer, Kelly Tripucka, and coach Chuck Daly.

Meanwhile, Spencer's surrogate father, Will Robinson, was also the assistant to the general manager and a Pistons scout.

"He thought that was a dream job for me," Spencer said. "I'm practicing one day—I got one practice—[and the Pistons players started talking to] me about L.A. and that was the end of it."

Spencer participated in one practice with the Pistons and was told not to come back. After being released, Spencer pleaded with Daly for another opportunity. He was 34 and saw his career slipping away. The situation in Washington tainted his reputation and the Pistons dealt him one final piercing blow.

His hometown team dropped him. After he helped put the University of Detroit on the basketball map, after he turned down several other schools to commit to his adopted home, Detroit essentially ended his career.

Over the years, Spencer said several players on the Pistons simply didn't want him around, especially veteran forwards Rick Mahorn and Bill Laimbeer, who would later be the nucleus of the Bad Boys in the late 1980s.

Spencer felt the Pistons players just didn't want an old man trying to steal their glory. During this time, he was clean. He worked out with the Pistons and then was brought into the offices of general manager Jack McCloskey and coach Chuck Daly and released. Just like that.

There would be no heartwarming homecoming stories. Spencer felt his abrupt ending in Los Angeles, along with players swapping stories about his heavy drug use and the prospect of a thirty-something taking shine away from a younger team, led to his dismissal.

Spencer knew that players, especially five-time All-Stars, aren't released after two days for basketball reasons. Once again, Spencer felt the NBA was again throwing him out on his ass.

"How can this happen?" he said. "I'm an All-Pro player. Let me go out on the road, let some people see me. That's what I was begging for. I was speaking to Chuck Daly—I ain't never begged for no basketball, man—but I'm sitting in there begging this man and it's such a degrading thing. Just let me go out and let me have some practice and go out on exhibitions."

The Pistons refused. Fifteen years after he was whipping the asses of Pistons players while at the University of Detroit, he wasn't good enough to be a Piston. The team was deep and young. Spencer would have been the oldest player on the team.

But he knew the slight was extremely personal. The court case, the lack of success with the Knicks, falling asleep at practice, the drug use, walking out on the Bullets.

"Nope, it's like [I'm] poison," he said. "Mr. Robinson was just crying. He was so hurt. It was a terrible thing and like, *Goddamn, the city that I saved and done all these things for and I can't get a fair shake here because of L.A.?* They kept saying, 'You might leave.' I didn't quit in Washington I had to take care of my family. They're thinking, *You might leave us again for your wife.* This lady was in a massive accident."

Years later, Spencer said he played in an All-Star Celebrity Game in 1987 in Seattle, and Milwaukee coach Don Nelson chased him around trying to have a conversation with him, to express regret for not signing him a few years before. Spencer said his body had healed and he was ready for one more chance. But his career ended after that one preseason practice in Detroit.

17

ROCK BOTTOM

A S HE DROVE BACK TO DETROIT, crossing the Ambassador Bridge that connected the Pistons' training camp in Windsor, Canada, and the city, Spencer pulled his Mercedes over in the middle of traffic. He stepped out of the car, walked to the middle of the bridge, and looked over at the Detroit River.

Perhaps it was time to end it all. Spencer knew his NBA career was over. His marriage was falling apart. He looked over the bridge, cars honking, deep in depression, and Spencer reflected on his mistakes and his regrets.

He was cracking under the pressure. He was riddled with depression and he contemplated suicide.

"It flashes back to coming up from down South, where everywhere I've been I've always had to be the savior," he said. "'You gotta save the Olympics. You gotta save Detroit. You gotta save the ABA, you gotta save the NBA,' you know? After one practice, that was a devastating blow. It was a thought in my mind—*This shit is so ridiculous. I should check out.*"

As he did with most of his setbacks, Spencer reverted to his Mississippi upbringing. He thought about a young neighborhood friend nicknamed "Brother Vann." One day, when Spencer was 11, Brother Vann was riding in a boat on the Yazoo River with two friends (one of who was Spencer's brother Floyd), when something went wrong.

Spencer's brother and the other boy survived, but Brother Vann drowned. It was hours before his body was found on the bottom of the river.

"What flashed in my mind was Brother Vann—he was the man who drowned in the back of my house in Silver City when I was a boy," Spencer said. "[The authorities] pulled him out of the water and they said [to my brother] Floyd and I and all the kids, 'Do not go look under that cover. Don't do nothing!'

"My brother had made it out. Earl Moore had made it out. We just had to go see that body… and when we saw that body we saw the shock on his face and the eyes bulging and I couldn't sleep for months."

The image of Brother Vann dead is something that still frightens Spencer. It scared the shit out of him.

"My mama crying on the bank," he said. "'Lordy, you saved my baby.' And she's crying with Mrs. Vann, because her son is gone. So it was like the whole town [out] there where they were dragging the river trying to find this man. And here I am a little bad-ass kid and I gotta see [the body]."

Fast forward to October 1984, 23 years later, and Spencer viewed himself as Brother Vann. He didn't want to be that body floating to the top of the Detroit River with his eyes bugged out and his doubters taking satisfaction in his giving up.

"When I looked over that rail and I pulled up and was stopped in the middle of traffic," Spencer said, "Standing there and I'm looking down… and people are blowing their horn [at my parked car] and I'm still looking down."

If he jumped—if he ended it all and killed himself—Spencer knew there would be haters, even at the pearly gates, waiting to unleash their tirades, ready to call him a quitter, a martyr, a junkie, a washout. He would go down as a loser.

"I know all these Black folks are going to be standing on the other side," he said. "We told you you wasn't shit and we ain't never gonna let you go from that drug addict shit and you shouldn't have sued the University of Detroit—you messed up Michigan. We could've had players forever.'

"Everything in my mind was culminating—the whole thing—all these Black folks waiting on the other side: 'We told you you wasn't shit when you came up from Mississippi.'

"So I didn't want to go over there to that other side of the river, and I didn't want to jump down there because of Brother Vann.'"

It was then that Spencer said he began to take his mental health seriously. He knew he was losing his mind, and the Detroit incident almost sent him over the edge. He needed to get clean, figure out what to do with his crumbling marriage, and realize that his basketball career was essentially over.

"What a crazy world," he said. "That's why my youngest daughter, Shaakira, is a psychologist and I can speak to my kids and my family about it. They never heard of nobody going to see a psychiatrist, because that's part of me and Iman, back when we were talking parting ways. We had to do marriage counseling and she suggested that we see a psychiatrist. So I love going to a psychiatrist—I could dump all that shit. I had so much shit and so much baggage. Time is up, you gotta come back next week."

Eunice was getting sicker, as she was losing her battle with cancer. But Spencer continued to lean on her for moral support during his travails.

"My mother was my biggest supporter, my biggest advocate in everything," he said. "She was just, oh God, my mom was like the shit. She did say, 'You let the Devil get to you after all them years and I warned you about the Devil. Didn't you read the Bible? What's wrong with you?'

"But I was always her baby, and she always told me she loved me the most—[though] she might have told all my brothers and sisters that. That was my girl until the end."

Spencer and Iman would actually take Zulekha to Mississippi to spend time with Eunice for the summer. Both would tell Eunice separately that they did not want Zulekha eating pork because of their Muslim beliefs. That was a difficult task for Eunice.

"She wanted to play in the cotton fields and hang out with the kids," Spencer said of his daughter. "She loved to walk around barefoot."

In an act of familial compromise, Spencer and Iman bought a stack of beef bacon for Eunice to cook for Zulekha.

"Hell yeah, she was feeding her pork," Spencer said. "We'd pick our daughter up every year and she'd be like, 'I don't want that beef bacon. I want grandma's bacon.' We didn't go off because it wasn't that deep. My mom couldn't wait for us to get out of her house so she could feed her that pork bacon. 'You gonna tell me what to feed my grandbaby?' That wasn't going to work."

Spencer knew his mother was sick, but she never revealed to him the extent of her ovarian cancer. He headed to Mississippi to be with her during her final days. Eunice was his only link to his Mississippi upbringing. With her there, it was always his home, despite so many painful childhood memories.

"I get angry sometimes talking about it, because that shit that happened in L.A. impacted her more greatly than it did me," he said. "You hear about the guys coming from up North, junkies, and they come down to Silver City and they get cleaned up for a while and then they go back up and get killed by an overdose. But I was the king of that whole land. And my mother didn't do anything outside of the Bible.

"So I'm like Moses getting high. That's a big statement there, but that's the reality. That's how much it affected her. There wasn't a Sunday that went by that the whole Shiloh Church didn't pray for me out loud. *Out loud, bruh.* When I got down there and talk to the people still, they'll say, 'Your mother was a praying woman. She prayed for you. We just so happy you okay. Look at you. Jesus sure did come by and save you.'"

Despite Iman being Muslim and also many of his friends, Spencer could never desert his Baptist upbringing. Throughout Spencer's life, his mother would always make sure to reinforce his belief, reminding him regardless of how far he was from home, he could always come back to God. He took that seriously, despite his faults.

"I can't just abandon Jesus, I can't," he said. "Because he done brought us through some shit. And me? Even though I love the prophet Muhammad and am down with it—that's some deep shit there, to be torn between both religions—but both religions were saying the same thing. They are living in a higher force, higher than yourself and better than yourself."

Spencer brought all of his family to Silver City and celebrated Eunice in her final days.

"At the funeral, we didn't cry," he said. "We had cried all of our tears in her final days. In our hometown, there was no way she could get chemo."

Spencer had to drive about 80 miles from Silver City to Jackson for Eunice to get chemotherapy.

"And she would come back with me sick as a dog," Spencer said.

One of the more pleasant memories Spencer carried was giving his mother that Cadillac and how that made her feel like the Queen of Silver City.

"She thought that was her 'Sweet Chariot,' that shit was for real," he said. "We would go and pick up all of the church members and bring them to church. It was just me and her. We had a good ol' fashioned time.

"There was so much pain as she was dying. I felt like I did my best. She lived her way and died like a queen."

Eunice passed away in 1980, right in the midst of Spencer's upheaval. In many ways, he said he felt he let her down, but he was always her champion. And she never let him forget that. Spencer blamed himself and his drama for her illness.

"That put me back because of the idea that worry and that pain brought the cancer more to light," he said. "That's how it manifested itself. But for me, to be out of it for that year and then to be shipped off to Italy—and normally I go home and see my mom, but I didn't get a chance that year. I was gone. And she would say, 'Into a foreign land.' That was some Biblical shit for her."

His mother would tell him, "Baby, I don't know how you've taken on all of the world. How could you be the chosen, baby, to take on the world? But you know the Lord don't make no mistakes! You've got to stand strong."

"That was through the court cases and the Olympics and everything," he said. "And yet, I made that one slip in L.A. and it was like all the good that I did in the world, this one thing destroys my marriage, my family, my mom. It's like Goddamn. I wasn't one of those players who felt like the NBA was a job. It was never a job for me. I loved ball.

"I loved the shit from the first time I fell in love with the game when I was 12. I loved that shit. That was my drug. I loved being competitive and I loved having the edge. I thought I could always outwork my opponent.

"I remember going against Moses Malone, we would be like, 'Oh no, you're not gonna outwork me now. You might outplay me but you're not gonna outwork me.' He idolized me. He put my name in his shoe when he was young because he said, 'I want to be like Spencer Haywood.'"

Spencer did not want to finish his basketball career on his back, but he did. The Pistons' release was the death knell. He spoke with the Bullets about coming back but they weren't interested either.

By then, under new commissioner David Stern, the NBA started a new media campaign with some of its premier players, such as Michael Jordan and Patrick Ewing, cautioning fans against the perils of drugs. The Lakers experience was still fresh in the minds of the league, especially since the Lakers would go on to win another title in 1982—with McAdoo, coincidentally—replacing Spencer as the veteran bench scorer.

"I didn't get a chance to have that epiphany, it's time, my shit is gone," he said. "I was ready to keep playing, but like I said, I believe in the Lord but it happened. I have to accept it, but I'm pissed off about it. I hated that it happened in Detroit, my home. Let it happen in Golden State, someplace, but not Detroit or Seattle."

At this point, Spencer didn't even have an agent, and he said he had no idea how to resurrect his career. So he let the desire just fade.

18

WHAT'S NEXT?

" **I** JUST DECIDED TO RESTART MY LIFE, and, *Hey, I gotta start trying to develop real estate*," he said. "My first project, which is still standing, is Circle Drive [in Detroit] with Coleman Young. And he was like, 'You gotta be out of your mind to take money out of your pension and put it in Detroit, at this time?'

"I was like, 'Sir, I don't have nothing else. I just want to do something for the city of Detroit and for myself. If I lose, I lose.'"

Spencer also purchased a mall in Salt Lake City during this final Sonics days and a few other properties during his NBA career. And that was not to be taken for granted. Spencer had trouble with the Internal Revenue Service over an old tax shelter he invested in during his Knicks days and the debt grew exponentially.

So in addition to all of the people who felt Spencer owed them, the IRS joined the list. He managed to sell a restaurant and another property to pay off the feds, but money wasn't plentiful.

"I called players and said, 'Can you help me out?' and them players slammed the phone down on me so hard, like nigga please," he said. "It wasn't about me asking them for money. I was just trying to get some legal help. Me and Will Robinson got through it and I maintained."

He also formed the Spencer Haywood Foundation, which teamed with the city of Detroit to bring back government contracts that had been lost by the city. Spencer returned to Washington—not as a player, but as a representative of Detroit to discuss those contracts with politicians such as senator and former presidential candidate Jack Kemp.

"We all brought the money back to Detroit because the politics at that time was pretty tight," Spencer said. "With Jack Kemp and I being former athletes, the Hall of Fame football player and me being in the basketball arena, we were able to hit a good strong relationship and try to make sure we get the money back to the inner city."

Spencer also worked with President Clinton's secretary of housing and urban development Henry Cisneros to bring funds back to Detroit for drug treatment programs, low-income housing, and new playgrounds to help spark the revitalization of the city.

The Brewster Projects and Herman Gardens, the housing developments that bore Diana Ross and many Motown artists, were cleaned up and made safer for their residents. And the Brewster-Wheeler Recreation Center, which hosted training for heavyweight champion Joe Louis and the Harlem Globetrotters, was refurbished.

"We had a lot of young people there that were dealing [drugs], so we had to get a safe zone," he said. "So I had to get peace with the guys who were using and dealing that this would be a designated [safe] location. 'So you have to be drug free in these 10 blocks here and the rest you can do whatever the hell you want to do.' The police was okay with it. We couldn't clean it up but we could give the kids some space to play.

"That was my baby for years because that was where my passion was."

And Spencer said he was glad to take part of his NBA pension and donate it to the rebuilding of old Black Bottom, a dilapidated area of Black Detroit.

"That's when I jumped into the idea with Coleman A. Young, when he said, 'You gotta be crazy to take part of your pension money to put it in here,'" he said. "And I was like, 'Sir, I could have easily put it up my nose. I'd rather do something for someone who has given me all the opportunities that I've had in my life, it started right here in Detroit. I want to do something back here.'"

Despite what happened with the Pistons, Spencer never lost his love for his adopted hometown. He would become a Detroit fixture after his career, and he wanted to help change his image and perception after the Lakers debacle by giving back.

"That was just a blessing; it really is to this day," he said. "It's a proud moment. And it was good for me to do that, but I was reconstructing my life. You can't reconstruct your life if you don't give and do good deeds. It was like my mother and the Bible. That's what I was taught. It was the reclamation of my life. It wasn't but a slip but it still gave me my pride."

Haywood even had a radio show on WCHB where he would help callers with their issues with recovery. The show reached as far as the northern part of Michigan, so his recovery audience was vast, and they would call in with their testimonies.

"I was in hog heaven, personally," he said. "It was good to be home. I had gotten clean years before but I was just sharing my thoughts and for people to have a celebrity coming on every week yapping about this on Saturday and Sunday, it was inspiring, but it was also giving me an anchor so that I would not go out and relapse."

What's more, Larry Johnson, the brother of Magic Johnson, helped Spencer with his recovery, as well as one of Isiah Thomas' brothers. Spencer became an integral part of Detroit's recovery community, embracing his challenge to stay clean and help others.

Being in recovery allowed Spencer to actually feel grateful for his journey. He didn't go broke. He wasn't on the street. He didn't lose family or friends. He still had a lot to be thankful for, especially compared with others who didn't have the fame or money.

"We thought we were some evangelists or something, trying to change the world," he said. "And we did. The beautiful thing about finding this purpose is that I had to humble myself. I couldn't sit around and talk about what happened with me with the Lakers? What, they don't respect me for what I've done? Why my name not on the ruling?

"You go into a 12-step meeting talking about that shit, and people will look at you like, 'Nigga please. What?!' People are living life and death and you're talking about shit like that? 'You got a Rolls Royce. You got a house in Canton. Boy please. Get some gratitude.'"

Spencer knew the root of his issues was his Mississippi upbringing and his resentment for the White power structure that tried to keep him out of the NBA and then kicked him out of the NBA. But he didn't want bitterness to destroy him, despite never receiving what he believed was the proper respect from the game he loved.

"I didn't want this to be destructive to me," he said. "Will Robinson used to tell us all the time, 'Those whom the Devil wished to destroy, they first must make mad.' So I can't be mad because the Devil is in here. I'm talking old-school Christian here. That's how we survived slavery—everything. Because we know certain things and certain rules that you go through, so I live by that old gospel."

But Spencer said it was a process. The bitterness continued to creep in, and it took therapy and soul-searching to dissipate it.

"It took a minute because I didn't get my just dessert as a basketball player," he said. "I thought I'd be able to write my ticket, like I earned this right to do this. I wanted to leave under the right circumstances. I had those issues and the biggest issue is what I had given to the game.

"How I went to these courts and battled and nobody likes me, nobody. All of these people I've created this wealth and worked for they looked at me like, 'Aww, what the hell? He's coming near me. Let me run the other way.' That's some tough shit, so I had to have help. Because the opposite of getting help would be to go and use again."

Spencer said he feared returning to his drug-abusing ways.

"I'm telling you, man, when I used, I was just sick," he said. "I was paranoid. I was depressed. I was angry. Everything bad that I could think of was happening. So I just didn't want to go that way. I just couldn't take that journey. Going to a psychiatrist, because I was able to [talk about my past] and then being able to do to the 12-step meetings—I would dump so much shit on the table that the people would be sitting up there listening to these basketball stories, talking about how much pain I got. And before you know it, the hour was up.

"I had to be good for my wife and be good for my kids."

19

DIVORCE, FATHERHOOD, AND GETTING SOBER

SPENCER AND IMAN HAD BEEN on shaky ground throughout their marriage, many times trying to repair their differences and pledging loyalty to each other. But the issues became too much to bear.

Iman's career was soaring as she stayed in New York and Spencer wanted no part of the big city because of the lure of drugs. During one instance, Iman accused Spencer of domestic violence, a charge he denied. In April 1985, he was ordered to move out of their Manhattan brownstone; he then headed for a rehabilitation center.

"My support system was in Detroit," he said. "If I [wasn't in] Detroit, I didn't have that support system. And she told me, 'You gotta hold the child until I get my next job finished up.' I realized, I got to step up here. We always had this idea that we would take care of each other, our family. That's our brand."

He and Iman had grown apart. Spencer admitted he was never quite comfortable in her modeling world and she was too much of a star to be limited to being a basketball wife or a housewife raising Zulekha. Iman had also moved in a friend that became her advisor and agent, and that created a complete divide in his marriage. Spencer felt outnumbered and unsupported.

"We were always going to be friends," he said. "And even when she was on Oprah, she said, 'Spencer ain't never hurt nobody but himself. He ain't that kind of person.' I was like, 'Go ahead, speak on it, my proud sista.'"

"I couldn't be mad at her," Spencer said. "Because she hung in there a long time. The shit was crazy. That was my warrior. We had this daughter and we always said whatever happens, we have to look after the child. We are the image of Black folks and we can't be out here acting no fool. We can't do that. We're more than just this married couple. We're like African and American on its highest order. This is royalty in America. A high fashion model and a great NBA player. It don't get no bigger."

The divorce settlement originally included Iman taking custody of Zulekha, who was seven, and Spencer getting visitation. But Zulekha had a troubled relationship with her mother because of her childhood weight issues and Iman's disapproval.

"Once I got the divorce finalized and then it became an issue of how we are going to do with the child because my kid was young," he said. "So we always talked about whoever wasn't working would share custody of the child, so that's how that worked out. So I ended up with a 12-year-old daughter and I'm like, *What the hell?*"

And since he no longer had basketball as an obligation, Spencer had time to embrace his fatherhood. So he, his mother, Will Robinson, Ms. Bell, a family friend, and his new girlfriend, Linda, helped rear Zulekha. Iman would visit Michigan and also take Zulekha back to New York for visits.

"Detroit was helping me raise Zulekha," he said. "It was really interesting, because when we first got together, my baby came on her menstrual period and I was like, 'What the hell?' So that this whole new thing—trying to get the right size, the right Tampax, cleaning up herself, and stuff like that—that drew me closer to my current wife. She was helping me. I was like, 'You're over here all the time, can you stay a little longer?'"

Meanwhile, Spencer had a second daughter, Courtney, from a relationship after his divorce. Courtney lived with her mother but spent summers with Spencer and his family as he tried to encourage his daughters to play tennis.

"She was the only one who stayed with my tennis program, through college," he said. "I have a relationship with her mom, my wife [Linda], Iman. I got four sisters too. So I'm a suck-up dude for these women. They always kind of agree with me. 'He ain't so bad. He's a good dude.' So everything was as smooth as it could get. But with the girls, they're all in competition with each other for dad's affection, so I used that to my advantage. I'm a ball player."

Spencer said fatherhood was something that he took seriously. It matured him.

"Ms. Bell helped me, she was the one who raised me in Detroit while I was away from my mom in Mississippi because she never came up," Spencer said. "But I gravitated to it. It's what I wanted to do and I kept having girls, so I had to submit. I didn't have no boys, so I wasn't going to be that tough dude. I was a girl dad."

During this time, Spencer realized he had to get completely clean, and rehab in the 1980s was an eye-opening experience for Spencer.

"The process of getting clean, I went to treatment," he said, "[that] was my first step. It was crazy. They didn't know what I was talking about. I went to Alcoholics Anonymous treatment, the cocaine treatment was under the radar. There were like two of us in the program for the first 28 days. And then I followed up because I didn't think I was ready to go out into the world."

There was a book Spencer used in rehab called *Coke Enders*, that was similar to the 12-step program in Alcoholics Anonymous.

"You gotta follow the whole principles and I like it because I love dumping my shit on other people," he said. "So I would just dump it in the group. I had a lot of shit in my heart. And it would always come back to that case—I don't know why. And all the shit I experienced in Mississippi growing up—racism, hanging, and all that shit. That always come back to haunt me.

"They didn't know no better. They were ignorant people. They did bad shit. And like Mama said, 'Don't be judging White people like that. Cause it's just the Devil got their heart. Don't judge nobody like that.'"

Spencer found himself talking more about his court case during his rehab sessions, especially with his psychiatrist. While the psychiatrist wanted to know the root of his issues and why, at age 30, he became addicted, Spencer kept discussing his childhood and the court case.

"My psychiatrist helped me a lot," he said. "I had a lot of regrets, you know? My wife, my kids. I didn't throw away everything, so we had a big house out in Canton, Michigan. I lived well and still living well. I don't have that kind of anger. I put so much into the game and I got so much out of it.

"I figured if I ever wanted to do something differently. All I gotta do is attack it the same way I attacked basketball. It's life skills and I've always attacked everything with the idea of making it better, not taking away from it. My mother always told me, 'You always keep your hands open, a lot can go out and a lot can come in. You're gonna get benefits from all the goodness coming in.'"

The one thing that hurt Spencer was that he couldn't save his family from similar addictions. His brother Andrew passed away five years ago after a long bout with alcoholism.

"It's horrible, a horrible death," he said. "That disease is in my family, so I try to tell my young kids, 'Hey, watch what you're doing. This one here is in the genes. Your dad done experienced it.'"

Spencer has always been his family caretaker, but he couldn't save Andrew and that hurt him deeply.

"You can't make somebody do something and it's hard for me to imagine that you can't step back [from drinking or drugs]," he said. "I know I was fortunate enough to do it, but I know it's a disease where some people can't. That's why I still go to meetings because I like to hear the stories. I like to feel the connection.… I see people all around; I'm always involved in that community. Because for the grace of God, there you go getting high, so I've got to keep my gratitude.

"You get cocky. You don't know what could happen. I just had an operation and they give you pain medication. I can handle them. But it's still dangerous."

Spencer admitted that bitterness crept in, especially when he kept getting disregarded by his NBA brethren. The impact of his courageous effort wouldn't be felt until 25 years after the Supreme Court case.

So throughout the '80s, Spencer Haywood wasn't a basketball pioneer, but rather the junkie who nearly cost the Lakers a championship.

Respect would take years to regain, but Spencer still had a daughter to raise and a post-NBA career to think about. He had pushed away the cocaine and realized he was still several years short of 40.

"I'm not begging for respect because I haven't been persistent in it, but how can you have this significant court case? Earl Lloyd walked on the floor as the first [Black] player out of all of them but Chuck Cooper was the first player and you got the Oscar Robertson Rule, the Larry Bird Rule, which is a modified version of my rule, but you don't have the Spencer Haywood Rule and that's the most important rule for all of sports," he said.

The Larry Bird rule allows free agents to sign new contract with the current teams without being restricted by the salary cap. In other words, it allows smaller market teams to keep their prized players without losing out to bigger markets because they can pay them a maximum salary.

"You can't have a Larry Bird Rule, you can't have an Oscar Robertson Rule and then you don't have a Spencer Haywood Rule, you just can't," he said. "And the young guys are just now learning about [the case]. Shaq didn't know that. Charles [Barkley] didn't know that. And when I tell them about it, they go, 'Wow, that's your rule.' I put so much shit on Chris Paul, I don't even want to tell him about it anymore. I always save my best stuff for the players association."

The Spencer Haywood Rule would allow players who have completed high school to be eligible to enter the NBA Draft. The NBA currently has the one-and-done rule, which mandates a player be one year removed from his high school graduation date before entering the draft.

"That's my dream right now," he said. "I don't know if LeBron [James] is the one to do it, but I thought he would be, [though] sometimes I think he's got too much going on. Chris Paul or Steph Curry or Kevin Durant should talk to Michele [Roberts of the players union] and say now it's time we named the rule as what it is: the Spencer Haywood Rule. And then I can die off happy. That's all I want out of this. That's all I ever wanted."

Spencer pointed out his case was *Haywood v. National Basketball Association*. And the league has gone through a series of names: hardship, early entry, one-and-done, to describe its draft eligibility rules.

"Why don't you just call it what it is?" he said.

There are striking similarities between Spencer and former St. Louis Cardinals outfielder Curt Flood, considered the father of baseball free agency. Flood was traded from the Cardinals to the Philadelphia Phillies after the 1969 season and refused to report, citing the racism in Philadelphia and the Phillies' porous record. He then sued MLB commissioner Bowie Kuhn for the right to be a free agent.

He lost. And he was eventually traded to the Washington Senators, where he played just 13 games before retiring. Flood was a Gold Glove winner in 1969 and in his prime, but he was done with the game two years later. Flood died at 59, exhausted from his struggle and unable to truly enjoy what he paved the way for, full free agency in baseball. That didn't occur until 1976.

"Me, Curt, and Muhammad Ali, we were in the courts, man," Spencer said. "When people like Stephen A. [Smith] talk about what

Curt Flood did… and I'm like, 'What the hell? I'm sitting here. I'm alive! C'mon! I'm here! Tell them about me!'

"But it's incumbent on the players association and the players. I did this for you. I've helped you guys make over six billion dollars. Do this one thing for me. That's all I've ever asked. But you know how we are as Black folks, we get in charge and we don't dig deep into our history at all sometimes.

"I got two spokespersons. I got Shaq and I got Charles."

At an appearance at All-Star Weekend in Chicago, Kevin Garnett, the first player to declare out of high school (in 1995) since Bill Willoughby 20 years earlier, called out Spencer for his contributions.

"I seen Spencer Haywood at the Hall of Fame [announcement] and he was the first person to have to go up and try to get into the draft," Garnett told an audience. "In 1970, he was the first player to ever get his rights to be able to play young, so we had the option to come out of high school and to do these things. Whenever I'm talking to Dwight [Howard] or LeBron or anybody that's in the game, I always make it a point to know their history, know what these people look like because without them creating this path for us, none of us would be here."

By the way, Spencer said he never considered going to the NBA or ABA out of high school, which would have been unprecedented. Will Robinson would not have allowed him to blow off college.

"He would have bopped me in my head," Spencer said. "Coaches used to hit you in the head and shit and hit you on the backside. He had a lanyard he used to wear around his neck and he would tap us up with that. He's an educator and I was living with educators. That's going to be there and I was planted at Detroit for four years, that was not a big deal to me because I loved the college experience."

Spencer said he was even being slighted by college coaches after his decision. He said they blamed him for the hardship rule and losing many of their most talented players to the NBA.

If Spencer was going to remain relevant in NBA circles and receive the respect and adulation he felt he rightfully deserved, he needed some help from some of the league's power brokers. David Stern was an assistant to commissioner Lawrence O'Brien when Spencer went through his troubles with the Lakers and eventually became commissioner in 1984.

Charles Rosenzweig was in charge of NBA entertainment and player marketing.

Both reached out to Spencer to help him with his rebranding.

"I was with all of the players when they would go to Europe; I would be on tour with them," he said. "They always kind of say, 'Spence, you did some great things for us so we're not going to support you like that but we're going to look out for you. We don't want no publicity. We can't show we're supporting you, but you're cool with us.'"

As for coaching, Spencer said he always thought about scouting because of his close relationship with Will Robinson, who had been a scout for years and gave Spencer all of his information and scouting books.

"He thought that was going to be the gig for me," Spencer said.

Before Spencer tried out for the Pistons, they offered him the radio-analyst job. But McCloskey reneged on that agreement once Spencer's tryout was a failure.

"That was one of my big mistakes because I should have taken that job but I just so wanted to play," he said. "So I turned down the job because I said I want to play. That was a big mistake. Not knowing the landscape and all of the baggage that I was carrying, I turned it down.

"Will was like, 'Take the job, and then keep practicing with the team. Even when you're not part of the team, just go out and practice with them. They'll see you.' But my ego, I said I wanted to play right now. 'What the hell are you talking about?' So a lot of that shit was me too."

Spencer stayed close to the game once he stopped playing. He couldn't help it. He was a mainstay at Pistons games at the Silverdome and The Palace.

"So there I was sitting there yelling and screaming, looking like a stupid fan," he said. "It was pitiful, embarrassing because I loved basketball. I can't give up. Right now I have the same problem. I'll sit up there and watch basketball for hours. And yelling and screaming and Linda asks me what's wrong. I don't know. I love it.

"I watch games. I look at stats and now the NBA gives the League Pass for all the old timers and I just watch all the games."

20

RESPECT AND RETRIBUTION

SPENCER KNEW HE COULDN'T CONTINUE LIFE as a single father with past bitterness. Gaining acceptance back into the NBA landscape would take considerable time, and Spencer said he realized that.

"You can't be around children trying to be angry and they're looking at you laughing, saying, 'What the hell is wrong with him?'" he said. "Well I did have a plan for my girls, but they did abandon my program."

When Spencer's daughters began developing—and he would later have three more girls (Shaakira, Courtney, and Isis) with his second wife, Linda, he approached Richard Williams, father of tennis legends Venus and Serena, to try to formulate a master plan to turn all of his daughters into star athletes.

"I am practicing my girls every day, we spent hours, got coaches on the sideline, I'm gonna make me some tennis players," he said. "And I was selfish about it because I was thinking I could travel to France, I could golf all over—like the way me and Iman used to travel—I could show my girls off. But that was my thing, go back to Italy, to the Italian Open, 'Hey, check this out.'

"Man, them girls said, 'Dad, we don't like tennis. We want to play basketball.'"

"Basketball?" he responded. "Are you crazy? Out of all the sports, I told you, you don't want to play basketball. So I switched up my game and I was training basketball. That was a good experience for me to go through because I was living vicariously through them and I am thinking about myself now. I could be at the French Open, Wimbledon, eating big fat steaks and shit."

Shaakira would play basketball at Northern Illinois University, while Isis played at the University of Illinois at Chicago. As much as he wanted to steer his children away from the game he once adored, he couldn't.

"I was angry because why would you want to play basketball and basketball did such a bad thing to me?" he said. "But it was what they wanted to do. It was their gene. I never talked about basketball like that. But I would take them to Pistons games, I ain't never disliked basketball like that. I was damn near a season-ticket holder for all my life in Detroit. That was my spirit. I never disliked the game."

The fact that Spencer's four daughters are all successes, he said, is his greatest accomplishment.

"That is my most proudest moment," he said. "This is truly a special thing. I had fun hanging out with those guys and I'm going to have fun hanging with them now."

His daughter Courtney gave birth to a son, Landon Spencer Haywood Bell, in 2015, while his daughter Shaakira gave birth to Golden, his second grandson, on January 1. He is banking on those boys reaching the NBA.

"All I gotta do is hang on for 14 years for the oldest to get to the NBA," he said laughing. "And he'll enter the draft using the Spencer Haywood Rule. I'm gonna walk up on that [NBA Draft] stage and walk them across. Spencer Haywood coming in on the Spencer Haywood Rule."

Meeting Linda reinvigorated his life, and the fact that she resembled Eunice wasn't lost on him. She was not a celebrity and accepted Spencer's shortcomings and him raising Zulekha as a single father.

"I don't know about the color of these women, because my mother is Blacker than me," he said. "I leave Iman and she's dark and then I look at Linda like what? You look like my mama too. And then I'm hooking up with her and I get this kid and I need some help. And she came along at the perfect time."

The past decade has brought Spencer the appreciation he desperately desired and felt he deserved. The Sonics retired his No. 24 on February 26, 2007.

"That was awesome, that was so great," he said. "It was so weird."

Spencer was presented with the game ball from that night's Sonics-Blazers game and it read: "We're retiring No. 24. The score of the game was Sonics 97, Blazers 73." It was a 24-point win.

"How could that happen," he said. "I got back to the hotel after the whole ceremony, I sit there and I'm looking at all this stuff and I feel this presence all around me, this designed presence because I had never been welcomed back to Seattle at that point. Everybody was hating me in Seattle for what I did and the image they had of me. They didn't know. They thought I was an angry person."

According to Spencer, Stern arranged the jersey retirement with the Sonics. It was some much-needed positive attention for the franchise, who were enduring hard times and would relocate to Oklahoma City less than 18 months later.

During an appearance in Seattle the next season, the Sonics' final year in the city, Spencer was flattered when rookie Kevin Durant recognized him and then told his teammates, "this is the Godfather here."

"That's why I call myself the Godfather," he said. "We never went into it any deeper and we never have. I always wanted to talk to him, like, 'KD, talk to me.' But we've never had that talk yet. We never had it. And when he was breaking records at Oklahoma, he was breaking my records. He broke another Spencer Haywood record, so he knows the shit."

Finally, Durant and Spencer were able to chat some when the Warriors faced the Sacramento Kings in a preseason game in Seattle in 2018. Spencer was invited by Warriors president Rick Welts, who was a Sonics ball boy in the 1970s.

Spencer said he was thrilled to be able to tell his story to Durant and Warriors forward DeMarcus Cousins, who left Kentucky after his freshman season to enter the 2010 NBA Draft.

"We had something special there," he said. "We never had a chance to talk. And you know I'm one of his biggest fans because of Seattle. I know he's Oklahoma. I know he's Golden State and all that shit, blah, blah, blah, but the shield with the Sonics are me, Gary Payton, Shawn Kemp, Fred Brown, Lenny Wilkens, the shield.

"And the sad part about my jersey retirement, do you know the next year nobody got a chance to see it."

Because the Sonics relocated in July 2008, Haywood's jersey was raised in the KeyArena rafters for about 14 months before the team moved. The Sonics became the Oklahoma City Thunder and did not take any of the retired Sonics jerseys to their new arena. So Haywood's jersey is on display at Museum of Industry and History in the Lake Union area of Seattle.

"I didn't get chance to enjoy one year of my jersey," he said. "Out of all the players that had their jerseys hanging up there. They got a chance to see their stuff and when teams come in and play they can come back and see it. But I never had that chance. There's too much shit that I get cut out of and it only happened to one player, and that's me."

The University of Detroit finally retired his No. 45 on January 30, 2016, 47 years after he played for the Titans.

"You gotta have patience when you're Spencer Haywood," he said. "If you don't have no patience, your ass will be messed up, because it don't make so sense. Nothing else makes no sense whatsoever. And you got Terry Tyler, John Long, Dave DeBusschere, everybody's stuff hanging in there [Calihan Arena] and I'm sitting in there looking like, *I built this shit.*"

When the Denver Nuggets were celebrating the 50th anniversary of their franchise last year, the PA announcer called out Haywood as the only MVP in franchise history. The Nuggets have not retired Haywood's 24.

"I'm like, 'Well y'all talking about me?' And I start looking to the ceiling [of the Pepsi Center] and thinking, *Waiting a minute then,*" he said. "Hopefully Dan Issel and Alex English are working on it and I'll see that jersey one day.

"Barkley said the Hall of Fame will never be complete until you have Spencer Haywood in it. I had been turned down twice already. [When he said that], I melted to the floor on my knees and said, 'Thank you, Jesus,' finally somebody stood up for me."

Part of Spencer's AA recovery was writing letters and calling friends and those he may have hurt over his journey. So some of his post-career years were spent making amends with former teammates, coaches, and adversaries. It may have not been all of Spencer's fault but he wanted to acknowledge his part in the dissension.

The reality for Spencer is that despite his mistakes in Los Angeles and leaving the Bullets in the middle of a playoff run, he had no real true enemies in the NBA. Those were against Spencer jumping from Detroit to the NBA had either softened their stance or died.

But Spencer wanted to repair his image, change the perception that drugs ruined his career.

"Everybody let it go, once I made amends," he said. "Because I do know recovery, I have to make amends wherever there is pain. And I let my deeds speak for themselves. That was really a warm-hearted feeling because I was so standoffish and hard and that was out of character."

What Spencer said he found out is that many of these people he felt he hurt had either forgiven him or just plain forgot what happened. There were times when Spencer had to even reminds his friends of his misdoings.

"When you calling people, they be in denial too," he said.

"'Why are you calling me? You didn't do nothing,'" some of those friends told him.

"No, I did this to you and I need to clear the air and move on," he told them.

"The second call, they call me back and we start talking about all of this good shit and it was a good period because you're airing out all of your grievances," he said. "And the person that you're doing [it] with, they're getting the joy of release too, because there was friction."

Spencer said he recalls many All-Star Games and other NBA gatherings where he interacted with former teammates and rivals and he admitted feeling awkward.

"It was uncomfortable," he said. "And when all of that was just washed away by asking for the forgiveness and, 'Hey, man, that's not me, and you know that's not me. This shit can take you down this road.'"

The apology process allowed Spencer to reconnect with Abdul-Jabbar, who embraced and forgave him for the issues with the Lakers. The two always shared an interest in different religions and they have become close over the years.

"Me and him, we kicked out all of our stuff," he said. "And that's been a good relationship."

Spencer said he also gained a greater appreciation for Bill Russell, his former Sonics coach. It was Russell who pulled Haywood aside and told him he had been making enemies with his Sonics teammates. And despite Spencer's anger, he said he respected Russell for his knowledge and respect for his talents.

"These people knew me back then," he said. "So they knew what I was doing [drugs] was out of character. Just thinking about some of the others guys that have been on the [retired players] board with me, we've been through some stuff."

As chairman of the Retired Players Association, Spencer brought in many former members, such as Dave Cowens, Archie Clark, and Oscar Robertson, and included them on board meetings.

21

TICKET TO SPRINGFIELD

BELIEVE IT OR NOT, SPENCER was placed on the Naismith Hall of Fame ballot beginning in 1988, five years after his career ended. But of course, he was passed up for decades for more worthy players, those with more eye-popping statistics and contributions.

Despite the crash ending to his career, Spencer carried Hall of Fame credentials. He won an Olympic gold medal, was a prolific scorer in college and the NBA, broke the barrier for hardship cases, he was an five-time All-Star, ABA Rookie of the Year and MVP, All-Time ABA team, and four-time All-NBA.

And as years passed from the Lakers debacle and Spencer reentered the NBA consciousness, his résumé began to improve. The Naismith Hall of Fame considered all basketball accomplishments, meaning the Olympic gold, his Trinidad State, and University of Detroit accomplishments were taken in account as well as his ABA season and off-court impact.

Eventually, Spencer began receiving outside support for his Hall of Fame campaign from journalists and his contemporaries. In 2013, Spencer said he had been tipped by someone in the NBA that he had been elected and his longtime agent, Al Ross, even called Fox Sports Florida to relay the good news. But it was an error. The Hall called him prior to the Final Four and told him he had again been left out.

By the next year, Haywood was resigned to being omitted and again he was. But he had bigger issues. Early in 2014, Spencer was having trouble urinating and underwent a series of tests. He had prostate cancer.

"I had the same process that Nelson Mandela had," he said. "I had been eligible for 27 years. Twice before I came up and it was really painful and you know you belong in and you see players that went in before and you're like, 'Man.'"

By the time the 2014 results were released and Spencer again was denied, he was preparing for cancer surgery. His thoughts had shifted to his health.

"My priority was on me, but the pain of falling short was still there," he said. "Being turned down again, I kept saying again to John Doleva [Hall of Fame CEO] that my mother used to sing this song in Mississippi, down in the old backwoods, 'The Lord may not come when you want him but he's always right on time.' It's gonna be mine the next year because I never did give up home because I knew I belonged there."

As for the prostate cancer, Black men are 50 percent more likely to develop prostate cancer than White men according to Sloan Kettering Cancer Center, and at age 64, Spencer was in the prime age group for contracting the disease. And according to the American Cancer Society, one in seven Black men will develop the disease.

Spencer considered his options of chemotherapy or surgery and he consulted with USA basketball chairman, former executive, and old friend Jerry Colangelo, who also battled prostate cancer. Colangelo told Spencer to get surgery and suggested a few hospitals, including the Henry Ford Cancer Institute in his native Detroit.

Spencer then talked with Dr. Mani Menon, one of the developers of the robotic prostate surgery, which uses a robotic system to place six incisions in the lower abdomen for better precision in removing the prostate.

He decided to get the surgery in April 2014, and when he arrived to check in at Henry Ford Hospital, his brother Roy was waiting there.

"Why you know so much about this?" he asked Roy.

"I had the same surgery," Roy said.

"Nigga please?!" Spencer said.

"You know how Black men are with health, we don't tell nobody about no shit like that," he said. "What's wrong with you?"

Spencer was in surgery for two hours and he was walking the next day and checked out of the hospital a day later. He stayed in the family home in nearby Plymouth for a few weeks and started walking briskly on a daily basis. Eventually walking became a daily part of Spencer's regimen and he also changed his diet, removing red meat and chicken.

Healthwise, Spencer was now ready for his next challenge. He was again on the Hall of Fame ballot for 2015 and the groundswell of support was increasing.

"God knew what was going on before I knew," he said. "Because if I had went up there with this on my mind, I got prostate cancer, man, I would have been a different person. I don't know how I would have been in 2014 but it was very heavy on my chest. My mom died of ovarian cancer but the Good Lord had it figured out."

In April 2015, Spencer was sitting on the couch in Las Vegas with his youngest daughter, Isis, again waiting for that call that would let him know if had finally been forgiven, finally been accepted into the ultimate All-Star team. Doleva told him he was in. Celebration ensured.

"We're jumping up and down, crying and laughing," he said. "When I told my brother Roy, he just broke down. We came a long way—Mississippi, Pershing High School, and to the Hall of Fame."

Spencer's past obviously kept him out of the Hall of Fame for years. But his induction in 2015 was basketball's way of final forgiveness. He had been clean for several years. Hundreds of players after him had entered the draft using the rule that he created. He had made amends with many of his adversaries. The good he had done far outweighed the hiccup in Los Angeles.

What was bizarre is when Spencer called some of his basketball buddies and friends to let him know he had been elected, many already thought he had several years before. It was one of the Hall of Fame's biggest oversights.

"Everybody that I'm calling, they were like, 'But you're in the Hall of Fame, years ago?'" Spencer said. "'No, I'm not.' You know a proud warrior never gives up his crown so everybody else was going in at that time but I was the king that day."

Spencer decided he wanted to be introduced by Wilkens, Bill Walton, and Charles Barkley, each who had championed his Hall of Fame cause in recent years.

"Me and Bill, we would get together when Seattle played Portland back in the old days," he said. "Burn a few [joints]. Charles Barkley put the nail in the coffin for me when he went on TNT and said 'It's a travesty that Spencer Haywood is not in the Hall of Fame. This should be the year the doors open.'

"And Lenny Wilkens is like my dad. He took me through the Supreme Court and everything else."

For that fall weekend in Springfield, the home of the Hall of Fame, Spencer was king. He was inducted with all-time greats such as Lisa Leslie, Dikembe Mutombo, Olympic teammate Jo Jo White, Tommy Heinsohn, John Calipari, and George Raveling.

Spencer strolled Springfield like royalty and accepted all of his adulation and appreciation with grace and humility.

Clad in a royal blue suit, Spencer spoke eloquently at the Springfield Symphony Hall for 12 minutes, detailing his career, thanking Robinson, tearing up when he mentioned saving his mother from picking cotton, and reminding those in attendance, which included several current players, that "I had game. It's not like I just did this Supreme Court thing. I had some serious game."

Looking back, Spencer said, "It was very special, it was like that first game I played in the ABA and the first game in the NBA," he said. "It was that kind of excitement, but also an excitement for the press because they kept pulling up things like, 'Wow, you were this Olympic hero.' They keep bringing up each one of these steps. So it was like me going over my life right there and the reporters and the media was just learning about me again.

"It was really, really exciting."

The Hall of Fame induction also allowed Spencer's children to be more familiarized with his playing career and accomplishments. Spencer had four of his five children following his retirement, so this was an opportunity for them to see first-hand his impact on the game.

"My kids were there, and they were like, 'We don't know this guy. This guy here?'" he said. "Because for some reason I never did talk basketball with them. My brother [Leroy] was there. Wiley Davis was there too. It was awesome. And I had to tell them I had some game. No, I just didn't go to the Supreme Court. I had some shit.

"And the Lord may not come when you want him but he's always right one time."

That lyric was from Eunice's favorite song, "He's Right on Time," popularized by gospel legend Mahalia Jackson. That song reverberated in his mind throughout the process. His mother was talking to him from heaven, telling him to be patient, the adulation will come.

"I'm not talking just Silver City but coming out of the cotton fields," he said. "There had to be a higher power in charge of all of this and yeah, I did break down. I cried because my mom wouldn't be there. Mrs. Bell, who had raised me in Detroit, she wasn't there. The man who wanted it so much for me, he would always talk about it and I would look at him like he's crazy, Will Robinson told me I was going to be a Hall of Famer.

"So yeah, I broke down and cried, that Sheraton Hotel was full of tears, full of joy."

Robinson passed away in 2008 at the age of 96. He had worked for the Pistons for 28 years after breaking barriers at Illinois State. Spencer was at his bedside in the Detroit hospital when Robinson perished.

"It was sad; he was like my father," Haywood said. "He had been with me through so much and he was one of the first people to believe in me. So when I got to the Hall of Fame and he couldn't be there, it hurt. It was hurt to lose those people who believed in you along the way and never wavered. So I cried a lot when I got into the Hall, thinking about my journey and the ones who didn't make it with me."

There had been times when Spencer felt slighted by his younger generation, many whom took advantage of the same law to enter the NBA Draft that Spencer worked to institute. When Spencer would spend All-Star Weekends meeting and greeting fans and talking to All-Stars about his journey, many didn't recognize him.

"I went to guys for years trying to explain who I was and what I did and they were [thinking], 'Aw man, that old junkie,'" Spencer said. "I'm telling you straight up. For that one year, that's how they would do me. Not about the guy who went to the Supreme Court, not the guy who saved America in the Olympics. All man, they just erased my shit to that level.

"So then they get a chance to see me, they see me in everything and they say, 'This has been the king all along.'"

22

A SECOND CALLING

HIS BRAND CHANGED AFTER THE Hall of Fame induction. The basketball world was reintroduced to Spencer. And his natural gift of gab turned him into a popular legend amongst the league's players, who before that were completely unfamiliar with his journey.

"It was a 180," he said. "I came back to being the leader for which I was before the incident with the substance abuse with the Lakers. But that took so much away from me in terms of credibility, everything. It was like everybody that wanted to get at me, they would always say, 'Well you got high. You ain't shit.' So it came full circle.

"That's why the Retired Players Association said, 'He's always been a leader so put his ass back in charge.' So when I go around, everybody is like, 'Hey, that's the king man.' So I got my crown back."

Spencer also said, however, there were former players and members of the NBA Retired Players Association who didn't want Spencer to serve on the executive committee because he hadn't graduated college. One of his primary opponents was former ABA player Marvin Roberts, who joined the Denver Rockets two years after Spencer did.

"What kind of abuse is that, man?" he said. "You wouldn't have a board if I hadn't did what I did for all these players. So that all these players would be members. So I went through all that drama and that shit for years... I just never thought Marvin Roberts, of all people, would do some shit like that. But he did it, right on the board. I'm sitting in there looking at the rest of the people."

At the meeting, former all-time great Rick Barry said: "Damn, if that's the case, I don't need to be on it either."

"That's when I said, 'Okay, Rick is my guy,'" he said. "Slowly, when all this shit decayed around me, the association, we were losing money. I started to think I should run this thing, because I see what's going on. And I can be the person to do it and lo and behold, the Lord put me in the right seat. And there I changed it completely and everybody said, 'That's what he did all along. That's who he is.'"

One of Spencer's greatest and most lasting achievements had nothing to do with scoring buckets or breaking barriers. It was working with the National Basketball Players Association to provide health care for retired players.

And Spencer said he puts as much emphasis on former players. Players from Spencer's generations and the 1980s made just a fraction of the money earned by today's players and many are struggling with earning a living and medical issues.

"The retired players, we were in shambles, we were like ridiculous," he said. "When I took over, I righted that ship. It wasn't me doing all the heavy lifting. It was me pulling everybody together under on banner and 'Let's get the healthcare that we need. Let's present this to the young guys and they'll agree with us and let's get a little increase on our pension.' Hell I didn't have to say anything, they were right away like, 'What do you want, man?' Nobody ever had to ask them."

The untimely deaths of Darryl Dawkins and Moses Malone just weeks apart in 2015 prompted the NBPA to begin performing heart screenings on former players during the Las Vegas Summer League. Many former players revealed they didn't have the money to pay for post-career medical issues that were caused by playing in the NBA.

So in 2016, the National Basketball Players Association passed a rule that provided health insurance for players who played at least three years. It was the first time a North American sports league had a healthcare plan for retired players. Also, the NBPA helped increase the pension for former NBA players and created a pension for former ABA players, who did not have a post-retirement plan.

"Everybody say they wanna be like the ABA guys—Julius, Moses, Spencer, David Thompson—but if you wasn't with a merged team, then you out," he said.

The ABA did not cover any pension plan for players who played in the league and weren't part of the four teams that merged with the NBA, so until Spencer became involved, former ABA players were completely unprotected.

"And when Chris Paul dropped that health insurance on us at $16 million per year, him and LeBron [James] and Steph Curry, the executive board," he said. "A lot of guys had to take their pension [payment] and a lot of guys are suffering. I said, 'You gotta make this happen.' They now have this respect for [me] like 'This guy went to bat for me.'

"Chris left school early. Steph left school early. LeBron, the whole executive board. They know! Because [executive director] Michele

Roberts, she tells them, 'Don't take Spencer Haywood lightly; that's the supreme sacrifice there.'

"I don't ever ask for anything for myself. All I want is for my men on the NBA Retired Players Association [to be taken care of], and you got guys like Nate Archibald who could have died if he didn't have a heart transplant."

Archibald underwent life-saving heart surgery in 2018 and was able to coach the Aliens team in the BIG3 Basketball League that next summer.

The NBPA heart screening also detected issues with former NBA center (and Spencer rival) Harvey Catchings. Former Spencer teammate Earl Monroe underwent needed hip surgery because of the insurance.

"We've got guys who will tell these stories of life and death here," he said. "Life and death. It's incredible. We got guys bone-on-bone with their knees, they couldn't even travel. Now they got these brand new knees, brand new hips. Them old niggas back on the golf course, trying to play basketball again. 'You 70 years old, cool out.'

"Now that's where my gratitude has been, with those guys and guys like Shaq. These guys are kind of promoting me. They used to run away from me, they thought I was crazy as hell, thought I was some old pimp, like Shaq said."

Spencer had to work to get the respect of the current players. It's difficult to find Spencer highlights on YouTube. His best basketball was played before the NBA's explosion with Magic Johnson and Larry Bird, so all he was to them was an old, well-dressed dude talking about the old days, before even some of their parents were born.

Current All-Star Paul George approached Haywood a few years ago and thanked him for his contributions.

"I didn't even know how to respond," he said. "I didn't know. I was like, *Paul George, I didn't think he would be the deep one.*

"I always had this thing in my head that it would be LeBron James [who] would be the one. I really did. All these years. That would be the guy who says, 'We're changing the name.' I don't know why I thought it, but I really did. I don't know why I have this kinship. When I watch him play, I have this eerie feeling that I'm watching myself. It's just so weird."

When asked if LeBron was the closest player to him that he's seen, Haywood said: "Yeah. [When] I was young and he was young. That's why my wife is always, 'You can't be so devoted to this man.' But shit, I can't do nothing about it. Sometimes with LeBron I get envious, because I knew I could have been this dude. If I had [known] about stats. If I knew how to take of my body. If I hadn't gotten messed up—aw, man, I would have been this guy. But that's a little bit of envy.

"And another guy I have big-time emotions with is Dwight Howard. I don't know why."

Spencer said he has a great deal of respect for today's game. He doesn't resent the salaries or the style of play because it's less physical. He believes the current players are more skilled because of technology and scouting advancements.

"You had to have fundamentals, your fundamentals and skill level had to be very high," he said. "Our generation, we just got out of slavery basically and we're playing basketball. There was a toughness that you can't imagine, but we didn't have no film or videos to study for a game. We had a projector, man. Today, they got all of these things. And I like our era and I say we was some hard-core players, but the game today, the shit is miles ahead of what we were doing. But I don't know how strong they are in the mental department. Could they have [handled] the kind of abuse we had to take? Play in the kind of shoes we had to play?

"I am proud of the game today. It's all evolution of the game. During the period of John Coltrane, Miles Davis, that shit can't be replaced. That was the best of jazz. That's us, and now you got Wynton Marsalis and those guys blowing to a whole different level—LeBron and them guys. They took what we had and expanded it."

Spencer has become a fixture at NBA All-Star Weekend and the league's Legend's Brunch. He is now a highly respected figure, and the NBA has kept Spencer busy with various camps and trips overseas to work with kids and teach a new generation the game.

"I just volunteer; I love teaching," he said. "The kids be like, 'You're so silly,' and I'm like, 'I know.' And one of the guys who was on the retired players board who came back to help was Rick Barry, because he said it keeps him young too."

"I never wanted them to treat me like some old beatdown junkie dude," he said. "So I worked out like a maniac. I always stayed in shape. I was always deep in prayer and meditation. I ate right and I always give love wherever I'm going. Where I am, I'm always spreading love, letting it all out.

"And when people see me, they just look me in the eye and reach out and grab me. They really do.

"Shit, it's like me and Bill Russell now. It's a new thing in the air. You should get some of this."

Throughout this journey filled with tumult, Haywood was able to maintain a comfortable lifestyle and provide for his family. Life after the NBA has been tough on several former players who lack the business skills or are beset with addiction or other personal issues. Haywood eventually moved Linda and his daughters to Las Vegas, where he was able to flourish with his business interests, while his reputation in NBA circles improved as years passed.

"I've been blessed—I really have been," he said. "When I look at my memberships—all the players I serve today—and I see all the crises, and the one thing [is] they all look at me, 'When you tell me through the Grace of God what you've been through, I can feel it.' So I have empathy for everybody."

For years, the court case pushed Spencer's limits, forcing him to be more understanding and tolerant, forcing him to accept forgiveness from people over the years that he swore he'd never forgive.

"It's like this rubber band, you don't know how much you're going to take and that band is going to break," he said. "I thought I couldn't take it anymore, but it stretched and it stretched. I hate to say I would attribute it all to me, that I never broke, but it was my upbringing in Mississippi that had me prepared.

"It's similar to the way Muhammad Ali, Jackie Robinson, and Curt Flood [were raised]—we're Southern boys. You see things that will not ruffle. It would be different for a guy like from New York City who never experienced that, never had to submit to going to colored water fountains—you can't go to the bathroom, you have to go out in the woods and there's a bathroom sitting right there. All of these things you just learn how to [adapt]. You know how Black folks are, we have one language for ourselves and one language for when we go out.

"I used all of that stuff. My experience was just dynamic in that journey. But I always wondered if I was going to break, and the people of Seattle kept me grounded."

And Spencer said he was finally able to make amends with his issues with Silver City. He traveled there in 2016, and was able to connect with old friends, family members, and other community folks from those painful days. It was therapeutic.

"I hung out with all of those Silver City people, all of the Belzoni people, they just thought this was the most spectacular thing," he said. "Mississippi gave me my anchor to everything that I know and that I have in life, my everything, my faith. There was bad, but I learned from listening to the blues from White and Black.

"They couldn't play in the [blues] place together. But they played in the backwoods, so we would all go and listen to guys do folks songs. It was like we were this secret society."

Those patchwork bands, the Mississippi culture, swimming in the Yahoo River, eating Mama's Southern cooking, were all elements that stuck with Spencer, and eventually he became proud of his roots, despite the racism.

"It was a beautiful experience as a kid, everything was an adventure," he said. "It was just a big-ass adventure. We'd get into trouble. They'd slap us around, but people do that everywhere. Hell, I look at today and think, *It wasn't so bad.* It gave me the strength and when I went through the Supreme Court and all the stuff that was going on, I always would go back [to my roots] in Mississippi.

"Even in those times of struggle, I would go back to Mississippi. I would play tennis on the courts out there and play all day long, play basketball, this little court in Belzoni. I integrated those courts. Blacks didn't play with the White tennis players."

Spencer refers back to those days, when Blacks were not allowed to play at the Silver City Country Club, just serve as caddies or servants.

"We were not supposed to play golf, play tennis, do anything at that country club," he said. "'Whatever you do, don't you dare touch no club or nothing!' We played with all that shit in the morning before everybody come over. And then we'd clean up the tennis courts with the leaves. The White kids knew that we were there playing, so they could come early too. Their parents knew what was going on and they knew their kids was playing with us.

"But in Mississippi you gotta keep a strong face, let other White folks know that [other White folks] weren't condoning this shit."

Spencer admitted that those days in the blazing Mississippi sun, picking cotton until his hands were bleeding, proved helpful later in life. Nothing could compare to that adversity, not the Supreme Court, not drug addiction, not being dismissed by the NBA.

"Working in the cotton fields was brutal work, it was hard work," he said. "But then when I got to my next level, when I started playing ball in high school and college and in the pros, everything I was doing, it worked. A kid pulling a sack of 100 pounds at 10 and 12 years old, my legs are built up so strong. I [had] more endurance than any other players. I could run. I didn't have a problem with running them to death.

"It was like I was in training and didn't know it. If I went through all of this in Mississippi, how could I lose it after this? It was like the anchor to everything I still do. That's when why you see me at the Hall, people think, *Man, I did a lot of shit to him, he's gonna be mad.* I got all that shit out of my head. I'm just like the happiest person ever invented. I try to work at that.

"People say, 'You're always smiling, you're happy.' And I say, 'I'm alive. I'm from Mississippi.' So between the two, Mississippi and Detroit, I had the best background of any individual."

Spencer has turned into a sage for younger players, someone who gives advice when asked. Younger players have so many more options than Spencer did. They can play overseas for a season after high school, attend college for one or more years, play in the G-League, or just workout for that year after high school. But Spencer tells them there's more to life than just playing ball. He's been retired for 36 years.

"You're not gonna have a full life just thinking about ball," he said. "When I went to Seattle, and even when I was in Denver, I went back to school because I just wanted to be around my peeps. I wanted to learn. When I went to New York, I got a whole other education right there on 125th Street, all of these great people I met. I was in plays and living it and learning it. You have to have that balance."

Spencer would speak to kids, many of whom had no idea who he was, at the NBA's Rookie Symposium, relaying his story and challenges, but also offering astute advice on their current situations.

"You're gonna have some obstacles come your way, but you need that balance," he said. "You gonna need to know some things. And that's why I look at the young guys. I explain, 'Whatever you do, don't take your career lightly and don't be a disruptive force on a team.' That was me in L.A.. So when I was explaining how I failed, I give them that example.

"Cocaine is so obsolete, I guess, I don't know. There's alcohol. There's a whole bunch of other shit out there that has the same effect. You have to have your guard up and you have to treat your body like a temple."

While Spencer said he filled some of his free time later in his career with partying and drug use, he strongly suggests the current players take up another pastime.

"Fill your time playing golf or tennis or something else outside of basketball," he said. "Go see as many plays as you can, learn about life, because it will carry you for the rest of your life to have that real solidness around you. And don't be like me. Don't want basketball all the time like me."

And there are times when Spencer still tries to run ball with the young boys. He'll go to 24 Hour Fitness in Las Vegas and run in a couple of pickup games. Eventually, age will always win.

"I always come out of there with a bruised knee or a shoulder all torn up," he said. "Because I can't play half-ass. When I play, I'm supposed to play real modest, [but then] these young bucks be jumping all over your back. And I'm like, 'Man, I can block that shit if I want to.' And then you block it and your knee is all messed up. It's a beautiful thing, basketball."

There are a few things left on Spencer's bucket list. He would like to get into broadcasting, and at 70 and with a lot of energy, he said he wants to coach. He played for some of the all-time greats: Robinson, McLendon, Russell, Holzman, Shue. He also spent time at the G-League Showcase in Las Vegas in December, working with some of the younger players and aspiring NBA coaches.

"I love these young guys because they think they're so clever and I want to be clever with them," he said. "They like me talking to them about all kinds of shit and plus it keeps me young and around basketball. Anything that keeps you alive and with basketball, I don't care how bad it treats me, I can't let it go. I can't not love it."

Spencer's legacy is complicated, but it remains incomplete. His primary goal over the next few years is to develop an NBA players retirement home for aging players in Las Vegas, where they can receive medical care, participate in activities, and have a comfortable place to spend their final years.

He said he's seen too many cases of former players unable to afford medical care, living in meager conditions, and dying with little money or assets to their name. Many of his NBA peers are dealing with serious health conditions and are unable to exercise or rehabilitate properly because of debilitating injuries from their playing days.

"It's my dream and I'm going to get it done," he said. "I'm going to need the help of the Players Association. I have some funds that I can start the project off and I hope the guys chip in and help me finish it. We're trying to put a Band-Aid on everything so they can survive."

Spencer's term as the chairman of the Retired Players Association expired in February 2020 and former NBA player and coach Johnny Davis was named as his replacement. Spencer said he wants to use his relationship with the current players to continue to improve conditions for retired players.

In the end, Spencer Haywood will be known for opening the door for young African American men to pursue their NBA dreams without being restrained by the NBA or NCAA. He set the course for the Malones, Garnetts, Bryants, Jameses, and Williamsons. He has been seeking appreciation for his sacrifice for most of his life, and at age 71, he finally feels at peace, acknowledged by those who he helped the most.

"Man it's feels good that I stayed the course," he said. "Even when times were really, really rough. I got a good-ass wife who really takes care of me and makes sure I'm eating right, sleeping right, and a good companion to be with. My girls, they are all doing well. Life is good."

Life has turned out the way Spencer wanted. He has reclaimed the respect and acknowledgment for his impact on the game. He rightfully received his induction into the Hall of Fame, and he is enjoying the fruits of his labor, the benefits of those scorching days under the Silver City sun picking cotton. Finally, he is reaping the emotional profits from fighting a battle that would benefit hundreds of young Black boys just like him, whose talent superseded their age and who earned the right to pursue their professional basketball dreams.

Spencer Haywood is a pioneer. Spencer Haywood is a trail blazer.

"All of them European players, Luka, Dirk, all of those guys, their freedom comes from a Black man, me," he said. "That's been one of my problems, I can't seem to reiterate how important this is. I know LeBron gets mad at me when I say, 'You're like $200 million richer because of me.' He gets really angry about the shit, but it's true. Don't be pissed. I'm just happy that I finally got the credit I deserved.

"The Lord done brought me through a lot of stuff, but I've always come out on top."